A HISTORY OF EDMONTON REAL ESTATE
& THE EDMONTON REAL ESTATE BOARD

RESPONSIBLE ENTERPRISE

A HISTORY OF EDMONTON REAL ESTATE
& THE EDMONTON REAL ESTATE BOARD

RESPONSIBLE ENTERPRISE

John Gilpin

Edmonton Real Estate Board
CO-OPERATIVE LISTING BUREAU LIMITED

Canadian Cataloguing in Publication Data

Gilpin, John F., 1947-
  Responsible enterprise

ISBN 0-9682695-0-8

  1. Edmonton Real Estate Board Co-operative Listing Bureau
Limited--History. 2. Real estate business--Alberta--
Edmonton--History. 3. Edmonton (Alta.)--History. I.
Edmonton Real Estate Board Co-operative Listing Bureau
Limited. II. Title.
HD320.E35G54 1997   333.33'06'0712334   C97-910976-0

Publisher: Edmonton Real Estate Board
            14220 - 142 Street
            Edmonton, Alberta
            Canada T5M 2T8

Cover Photo: City of Edmonton Archives EA-63-11
            Jasper Avenue traffic problems
            CIRCA 1914   MᶜDERMID STUDIOS

Editor: Barbara Demers
Design: Graphic Design Limited
Cover Design & Book Layout: Liz Bolduc
Typesetting Output: Real Estate Weekly
Printing and Binding: Quebecor Jasper Printing, Edmonton, Alberta, Canada

♻ Printed on recycled paper.

The Edmonton Real Estate Board gratefully acknowledges the support
received from the Alberta Real Estate Foundation toward the publication of
this history book.

Printed in Canada

Foreword

A decade ago various suggestions were made regarding the desirability of producing a history of the Edmonton Real Estate Board (EREB). During the next several years a number of members, who might have been in the best position to provide details about the formative years of operations and accomplishments, were no longer available due to illness or death. It was understood that there were few written records and photographs of the early years and that we would be largely dependent on a verbal and anecdotal recounting of past events. The realization, that with every passing much of this information was now lost to us, spurred the efforts to formally undertake the project.

In 1993, the Board of Directors authorized the *Ad Hoc History Book Committee* with the task of producing a budget, locating and engaging an author and establishing the parameters of the project. From the beginning, the Committee agreed that the history of the EREB was intertwined with the economic development of the Edmonton area and the real estate activity that responded to it. It was therefore decided that reporting on the earliest real estate development and sales activities would provide the proper foundation for subsequent events. The theme of the book would be developed around the parallel growth of the community and the real estate industry.

Our History Book Committee members were novices to publishing. We had no inkling that this 'temporary' committee with a single task would labor for five years to produce this tome. Early responsibilities included arranging interviews for the author and directing him to likely sources. Part way through the process a treasure trove of early documents and photographs was discovered in the far reaches of the Board basement. This not only provided confirmation of the recollections of the senior and former members, but added documents and detail not available from any other source.

Draft after draft of the manuscript was read. Suggestions were made for additions and revisions. As the document took form, the editing function began. Committee members, from their combined years of active participation in Board affairs, were responsible for fact and sequence of events. The Directors were informed periodically of our progress (or lack of it) and were always supportive and encouraging.

As the years passed it became evident that, in our naive enthusiasm, we had launched a project that had become all consuming and self-perpetuating. Observations and inquiries from members became more pointed as completion dates came and went with disconcerting regularity. This steeled the resolve of all those involved to see it through to fruition. The end product would be, hopefully, not only authoritative but unique, enlightening and, yes, even entertaining.

It is inevitable, in an undertaking of this scope with such a wide variety of sources, that some events and people might be omitted. This we regret and request your indulgence. The book concludes with 1995 activities. This is no reflection on the activities of those that have made outstanding contributions to the function and accomplishments of the Board since then, but rather positions them to be the opening chapters in subsequent volumes.

So many people contributed to this project including members and directors – past and present – the author, editor, Committee members and Board staff. It is hoped that they, and you, will feel this has all been worthwhile; and that knowing where we have come from will provide a guide to where we are going.

R. Harvey Galbraith
September 8, 1997

Acknowledgements

It is nearly impossible for a project of this scope to come together without the input and hard work of a great number of people. The Edmonton Real Estate Board wishes to acknowledge the following individuals and organizations for their many contributions.

Author and historian, Dr. John Gilpin, for his diligent research.

Editor, Barbara Demers, for editing 'above and beyond the call of duty'.

Life Member, Norm Winterburn, who lived the history and recounted it for us.

EREB History Book Committee members: Chairman Harvey Galbraith, Sherry Belcourt-Darby, Graham Downey, and Alec Fedynak, for their preseverance and ongoing commitment throughout this important project.

Public Relations Manager, Geri Myers, for her guidance and able assistance.

Public Relations Assistant, Elvera Walde, for recording the Committee's many and often lengthy, deliberations.

Real Estate Weekly Publisher, Dave Robb, for valued production assistance.

EREB Executive Vice-President, Ron Hutchinson, for his ongoing support.

All Past Presidents and members of the EREB who provided pertinent information for the book.

The Alberta Real Estate Association and the Canadian Real Estate Association, for open access to their historical records.

The Alberta Real Estate Foundation, for granting additional funding to allow wider book distribution beyond our membership.

Table of Contents

Introduction

esponsible Enterprise: A History of Edmonton Real Estate and the Edmonton Real Estate Board traces the history of the Edmonton Real Estate Board from its earliest beginnings to its present-day accomplishments. From 1909, people have sought to create an organization that would be helpful for its members and the public. Objectives evolved over time. The present goals of the Edmonton Real Estate Board are to:

- improve the efficiency of the industry through such practices as providing a multiple listing service
- protect the operation of the free market
- promote the self regulation of the industry
- maintain the integrity of the industry by establishing and enforcing a code of ethics
- promote the education of its members
- organize social activities for its members
- benefit the community through various charitable activities
- recognize peers who excel in the profession
- advise governments on the appropriate regulations to protect both members of the real estate industry and the public

Real estate and real estate agents have played an important role in Edmonton's history since the city began its transition in the 1870s from a fur trade post to a modern urban community. Chapter One (1870-1899) looks at the Hudson's Bay Co. (HBC), which became the first "land seller" in western Canada, when it engaged in the biggest land transaction in Canada's history. After that sale, land became available for people to buy privately. Soon after, encouraged by the Dominion of Canada, settlers slowly began to arrive in the area. Delays in surveying their claims and granting titles led to the creation of a settlers' rights movement. It protected the community from "claim jumpers." Edmonton citizens dealt directly with anyone who tried to develop land whose claim to the land was not recognized by the community. In 1882 buildings under construction were thrown over the edge of cliffs by enraged citizens.

By 1880 local citizens' hopes and expectations regarding the arrival of the Canadian Pacific Railway (CPR) led to the first land boom. The community was encouraged by the Hudson's Bay Co. to believe that the Edmonton Settlement was on the mainline of

The transition of Edmonton from a fur trade outpost to a modern urban community is symbolized in the photograph below, which shows the remnants of Fort Edmonton with the new legislature building in the background.
(Glenbow Archives, NC-6-234)

the CPR. Events, however, would show that the HBC was more interested in selling land at inflated prices than in the long term promotion of Edmonton's development.

Chapter Two (1900-1913) discusses the formation of the Edmonton Real Estate Exchange in 1909. While the Exchange did not last long, it laid the foundation for the future of organized real estate. It was established during a boom sparked by the actual arrival of transcontinental railways. The Canadian North Railway (CNoR) arrived in 1905 and the Grand Trunk Pacific (GTP) in 1909. The CNoR was provided with land for a terminal while the GTP was given a cash bonus and tax concessions.

Settlers in search of farm land were important customers for Edmonton's early real estate agents.
(Glenbow Archives, NC-6-576)

Land speculation and grossly inflated prices and plans soon followed. Neither the real estate industry nor the government dealt with the problems that arose.

The First World War and the interwar period are the topics of Chapter Three (1914-1939). This period was another cycle of boom and bust. The economic expansion of the late 1920s was not reflected in the re-emergence of land speculation. The recovery was, however, sufficiently strong to prompt the real estate industry to create the Edmonton Real Estate Association. Its main accomplishment was bringing about the passage of the first legislation requiring the licensing of real estate salesmen. In this way the industry hoped to protect real estate agents and the public alike.

However, its effectiveness as an industry association was limited by the onset of the Depression. The Association also did not offer any real benefits of membership, and so most real estate agents had little reason to join.

Chapter Four (1940-1950) discusses World War Two, and the economic developments of that period. The Second World War was a mixed blessing for the real estate industry. It ended the Depression but it brought about the regulation of the economy. The restrictions on the real estate industry were the catalyst for the organization of national and provincial associations. The one restriction which was of particular concern was the clause in the Veterans' Land Act, which prevented real estate agents from charging commissions on land sold to veterans.

Thirty years of success and expansion followed for the real estate industry in Edmonton. The subject of Chapter Five (1951-1981), is the "golden age" for real estate in Edmonton. The achievements in the golden age included the creation of the Edmonton Real Estate Board Co-operative Listing Bureau, which superseded the Edmonton Real Estate Association as the vehicle for organized real estate in Edmonton. The Board acquired permanent offices, culminating in the building of its present facilities. A full time staff was also hired to oversee the wide range of new services offered, which made membership in the organization desirable for any real estate professional.

Chapter Six (1982-1995) looks at the decade following the 1982 recession and the effects it has had on the real estate industry. The cancellation of some northern developments projects, the implementation of the national energy policy, and the downsizing of government has meant another adjustment for the Board and its members. On the positive side, an ever-increasing use of computers and other technologies, and a greater demand for professionalism and education for its members has meant that the industry has continued to grow and change.

CHAPTER ONE

Real Estate and the Birth of Edmonton 1870-1899

*P*roperty rights and real estate preoccupied Edmontonians during the period from 1870 to 1899 when Edmonton made its transition from a fur trade outpost to a modern urban community. Everyone seemed involved in the process of making and protecting land claims and agitating for the necessary policies to speed up land transfers. Surveys of the Hudson's Bay Co. Reserve and individual land claims had to be made and deeds issued. When the Dominion Government delayed in dealing with land claims, a settlers' rights movement began where citizens of Edmonton protected their perceived property rights with vigilante action.

The Dominion Government eventually responded by creating the North Alberta Land Registration District, and appointed Thomas Anderson to be the first Dominion land agent in Edmonton. He regulated land transfers, issued titles, and registered subdivision plans so that an orderly transfer of property could take place. The North Alberta Land Registration District continues to operate on the basis of the Torrens system of land registration.

Almost as important to the citizen's actual land claim was the land's potential for increasing in value. Up to 1900, the Canadian Pacific Railway and the Calgary and Edmonton Railway were the most potent influences on property values in the Edmonton real estate market. Railway companies could cause a boom simply by indicating their intention to build through to a particular location. The first Edmonton real estate boom of 1882 is evidence of this influence.

This interest in real estate did not, however, produce a sufficient number of land transactions up to 1900 to create the need for a separate industry. Real estate was handled by insurance agents or by general merchants who also purchased grain and sold merchandise to settlers.

Fur trade post to urban community

Fort Edmonton and the land surrounding it was officially under the control of the Hudson's Bay Co. by virtue of its 1670 royal charter from England. The end of Hudson's Bay Co. rule came with the transfer of Rupert's land to the new government of Canada in 1870.

After 1870 the Hudson's Bay Co. had a 3,000-acre Reserve left in the Edmonton area. The precise location of the Hudson's Bay Co. Reserve's boundaries were not known until 1876 when it was officially surveyed by the HBC.

The Hudson's Bay Co. Reserve was bounded on the south by the North Saskatchewan River, on the west by 121

Fort Edmonton (pictured here in 1879) declined as the centre of commercial activity after the transfer of Rupert's Land to Canada in 1870.
(City of Edmonton Archives, EA-10-71)

Street, and on the east by what is now 101 Street. It extended as far north as 122 Avenue.

Creation of the Edmonton Settlement

Reverend George McDougall was one of the first men to claim land privately in the Edmonton area. He arrived in June 1871, and claimed land on behalf of the Methodist Church to the east of the Hudson's Bay Co. Reserve, while his son David claimed the adjacent property. By 1873 a church and house had been built on these properties, and so began the building of a town outside the walls of Fort Edmonton.

Employees of the Hudson's Bay Co. also made land claims at this time. Unlike the Methodist property, their lots were located on both sides of the river. An official survey was carried out in 1883 and the Edmonton Settlement, as this survey area was called, consisted of forty-four lots. The process of subdividing the Edmonton Settlement into urban land began in 1879 when Colin Fraser, an employee of the HBC, sold a small portion of his claim to Frank Oliver for $25. In February 1881, he sold a further two lots, fifty by one hundred feet in size, for $890.

The river lot or settlement plan was a rural form of land survey used to accommodate existing communities in the west, often those established by Metis.

Edmonton's first land boom

The Hudson's Bay Co. was the first land owner to undertake the large-scale subdivision and promotion of its property. On October 29, 1881, the company announced the creation of

The Edmonton Settlement was made up of river lots along both sides of the North Saskatchewan River.
(City of Edmonton Archives, EAM 85)

Malcolm Groat was one of the Hudson's Bay Company employees who claimed land outside Fort Edmonton, thus initiating the creation of the Edmonton Settlement. He claimed land west of the Hudson's Bay Co. Reserve, which became River Lot two in the Edmonton Settlement.
(Provincial Archives of Alberta, B 7118)

the "City of Edmonton." Their advertisement in the *Edmonton Bulletin* said the townsite was at the centre of the gold, coal, timber, and mineral region of the great North-West, and was surrounded by the richest wheat-producing country in the world. The most important aspect of the new townsite, it said, was that it was on the projected Saskatchewan branch of the Canadian Pacific Railway (CPR).

The Hudson's Bay Co.'s high expectations were shared by Frank Oliver, the publisher of the *Edmonton Bulletin*, Alberta's first newspaper. He wrote in his paper: "*There is a possibility that the syndicate have decided to build the CPR via Edmonton, crossing the river here, and uniting with the H.B.Co. in building upon their property the metropolis of this far North-West. If this surmise should prove correct, and it is at least reasonable, all the booms that have taken place yet in Manitoba or elsewhere will be nothing compared to that which the tumble-down walls of Fort Edmonton will see during the next year or two.*"

After its advertisement appeared, the Hudson's Bay Co. called a public meeting to explain its plans and invite participation in designing certain aspects of the town. Terms of the land sales were one-third cash and the balance in two equal instalments. Buyers were required to erect a building within eighteen months from the date of purchase on at least every second lot. Lots were free for schools and churches.

Plan B, the subdivision that covered the southern portion of the Hudson's Bay Co. Reserve, contained 2,137 lots.

Edmonton's first legal subdivision found a ready market when

offered for sale. The *Edmonton Bulletin* reported on February 3, 1882, that the moment the land went on sale "*there was a rush for lots that would have surprised even a Winnipeg auctioneer, and in three or four days $12,000 worth, or about 400 lots were sold subject to building conditions.*" The selling price averaged $32 per lot. Hudson's Bay Co. Land Commissioner Charles Brydges then assumed control of future land sales because he considered the price too low. Brydges' pricing strategy was to withhold the land from the market and to deal only with Winnipeg or Eastern Canadian investors. This approach brought immediate results when the Scottish, Ontario, and Manitoba Land Co. purchased 300

The central business district of Edmonton in 1890 developed east of 101 Street in order to avoid the Hudson's Bay Co. Reserve.
(Provincial Archives of Alberta, B 4756)

The Methodist church property was located at the corner of 101 Street and College Avenue in 1902. This is the current site of McDougall United Church.
(Provincial Archives of Alberta, B 3677)

lots at $110 per lot. This sale prompted enquiries about Edmonton land from people in Toronto, London, and Hamilton. Given the rising demand, Brydges was able to raise the price as high as $250 for lots in choice locations. Even at these inflated prices, about 500 lots were sold.

The interest in Edmonton lots prompted Brydges to subdivide additional land. It was sold by public auction. The Hudson's Bay Co. auction in Winnipeg was two days of frantic activity where about 500 people participated in one day alone. Total sales of property during this auction amounted to between $250,000 and $300,000.

Interest dwindled in the company townsite, however, by the spring of 1882. The CPR had decided on a southern route. With the end of the boom, the Hudson's Bay Co. lost interest in their Edmonton property, as did most people who had purchased land during the boom. In Brydges' opinion: "*The great bulk of the sales made at Edmonton will not be carried out. There is no railway projected at present to Edmonton, and until that is done the sale of lots will not amount to anything.*"

Frank Oliver, however, disagreed. In the *Edmonton Bulletin* on June 17, 1882, he wrote that:

Outside of the boom the prospects of Edmonton are second to those of no place in Manitoba or the North West except Winnipeg. The boom as far as it has gone left a large amount of money here of which every dollar has been invested and if it has burst utterly and lots can now be sold in Winnipeg for a cent a piece that matter will concern very few people here. They have not been in the real estate business. The boom started suddenly and went ahead too rapidly for them to invest.

The collapse of Edmonton's first land boom did not stop the subdivision of land. It simply shifted the activity back to the river lots in the east where the town of Edmonton had begun.

Land claims

The land claims of the Hudson's Bay Co. and others during the 1870s and 1880s led the settlers to request an official survey of the settlement and recognition of their claims. On January 15, 1880, Frank Oliver warned that if the land claims issue was not solved then it

This is a map of the Town of Edmonton at its incorporation in 1892. The Hudson's Bay Company subdivision, which caused all the excitement in 1881, is included.

(City of Edmonton Archives, EAM 17)

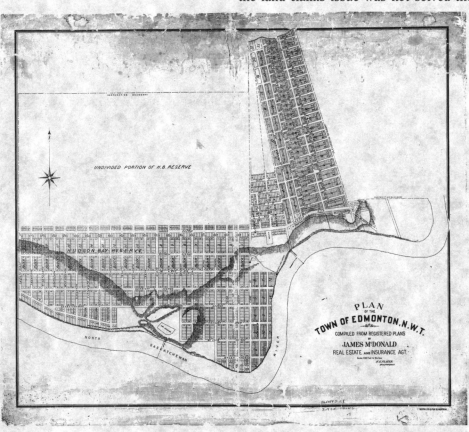

would create discord in the community. His prediction came true on February 4, 1882, when the community discovered that L. George, an American working as a clerk in the Villiers store, was trying to take over land

was ordered by the Court to pay Bannerman $40 to cover the cost of the lumber destroyed. Following these events, the government moved to survey the individual land claims and issue titles.

Calgary and Edmonton Railway Station was constructed in 1891. It was replaced in 1907 by the brick structure currently being used by the CPR.
(Provincial Archives of Alberta, A 2996)

claimed by Thomas Anderson. George had driven in boundary stakes around the property he claimed and hired carpenters to build a house at this location. The community saw this as a test case for the security of other claims that still did not have the benefit of a legal survey and official title. On the morning of February 6, 150 people gathered and asked George to remove the building. Upon his refusal, the crowd overpowered him, and the house was dragged to the river bank and thrown over the edge.

Following this episode a vigilante committee was organized to protect claims in the future. No sooner was it formed than J. H. Bannerman wrote to the vigilantes that he intended to occupy the former mission lot that was claimed by Matthew McCauley. His house was dealt with much as George's had been. Bannerman, unlike George, was not prepared to suffer in silence. Warrants were issued for the arrest of the seven people involved in the "house moving." The trial took place on June 15, 1882. All defendants were acquitted since it was proven that McCauley had the right to the land. Bannerman's civil suit against McCauley was heard the next day. McCauley

The Calgary and Edmonton Railway

In 1890 the construction of the Calgary and Edmonton Railway prompted Frank Oliver to write an editorial entitled "Brightening Prospects": *"Ever since work began on the Calgary and Edmonton Railway, with every mile added to the grade, outside interest in this district has risen and every week the arrivals of land prospectors has increased. Land is being taken up in all directions with the town of Edmonton as the centre, and in another year, from present appearance, the taking which are now by quarters or sections will then be by township and blocks of townships."*

Construction of the Calgary-to-Red Deer section began on July 8, 1890, and was completed by early December. By March 28, 1891, the Calgary and Edmonton Railway Co. had registered the plans and profile of the line to approximately two miles south of the banks of the North Saskatchewan River. The *Edmonton Bulletin* observed that this *"ensures the location of the terminus at Edmonton, although what is to be the actual site of the terminus is yet a secret, but will be made known in a few weeks at most."*

The *Edmonton Bulletin's* confidence that the Calgary and Edmonton Railway would cross the river ended when route information was made public in March 1891. At the same

Whyte Avenue, seen from the CPR tracks at the turn of the century, was the main street of Strathcona. It was incorporated as a separate town in 1899.

(Provincial Archives of Alberta, A 3002)

time that these documents were being filed, the Calgary and Edmonton Railway Co. was secretly acquiring land for the new terminus on the south side of the North Saskatchewan River. The new townsite was originally called South Edmonton but the name was changed to Strathcona when it was incorporated as a town in 1899. The Calgary and Edmonton Railway Company created a new townsite rather than crossing the river into Edmonton in order to monopolise the benefits of future land sales.

In March of 1891 the company had negotiated agreements with Joseph McDonald, owner of river lot eleven, Frederick H. Sache, owner of river lot fifteen A, and Alexander McDonald, John Cameron, and Malcolm and Sarah McLeod, owners of the southern 103 feet of river lot seventeen plus the fraction west half of section twenty-eight. An agreement dated April 6, 1891, covering river lots thirteen and fifteen completed the land arrangements for a townsite by the Calgary and Edmonton Railway Co.

The terms of these agreements for all parties were the same: the owners agreed to provide the Calgary and Edmonton Railway Co. with sufficient land up to a maximum of thirteen and one-half acres for right-of-way and station grounds, plus a half interest in the remaining portion of land, in return for a

station and engine shed built by the railway.

The agreements stated that the railway company would survey the townsite with the cost shared equally among the parties. Once the survey was completed, the land could be divided or an agent appointed for the joint sale of all townsite properties.

The Calgary and Edmonton Railway Co. moved quickly to fulfil the terms of the agreement when the steel reached the location of the proposed townsite in July 1891. By July 25, the survey of the townsite had begun.

Plan I, registered in the Land Titles Office on September 25, 1891, was Edmonton's first south side subdivision.

The streets at the new townsite were named by the Calgary and Edmonton Railway Co. to honour railway and local officials, the original land owners, and prominent citizens of Edmonton and area.

Streets named after railway officials included Whyte (82nd) Avenue and Niblock (105th) Street. Anderson (81st), Sache (88th) and McDonald (83rd) avenues were named after three of the original owners of the townsite land. Main (104th) was the main street running north and south. West (103rd) and East (102nd) Railway streets were located to the west and east of the railway right-of-way. An avenue was even named after Frank Oliver (86th), despite his intense dislike of the Calgary and Edmonton Railway.

Edmonton's first real estate agents

Despite the flurry of activity in 1881 and 1891, the comparatively small number of land transactions in the Edmonton market before 1900 was not enough work in itself for a group of real estate agents. They worked at other jobs, including the fur trade and general merchandise. This group included Walter Scott Robertson, Alexander MacDonald, and John Cameron, who were partners in the general merchandise and trading company called A.

MacDonald and Company. When Robertson, MacDonald, and Cameron arrived in Edmonton in June 1882 they invested about $30,000 in an interest in river lots twelve and fourteen in the Edmonton Settlement and other property at Fort Saskatchewan. The property acquired in Edmonton was subdivided in November 1882. The subdivision created 1,594 lots, generally thirty-three by one hundred feet in size.

Other pioneer merchants who also sold real estate as part of the company operations were McDougall and Secord, and William Wilke, whose general store was located in South Edmonton.

The first real estate agency to advertise its presence in the community was operated by Messrs. McKay and Blake, who in the January 7, 1882, *Edmonton Bulletin* invited *"parties in the East wishing to invest in real estate in Edmonton or vicinity . . . to correspond with . . . them."* They remained in business only a short time. That same year Blake became auctioneer and farm equipment salesman while McKay left the area.

In August 1882 William Stiff advertised that he bought and sold property on commission, collected accounts, managed estates for nonresidents, and furnished information to intending settlers. He continued in this line of business until 1884.

The real estate agent active for the longest time in the 1880s was Stuart Mulkins, who arrived in the Edmonton district in the fall of 1881 as the census commissioner for the Edmonton and Bow River districts. By July 1882 he had established himself as a notary public and conveyancer. Initially he concerned himself with the location of coal claims and timber limits but by December 1882 he had become

the sole agent for the subdivisions in river lots ten, twelve, and fourteen. He moved to Red Deer in 1887.

By 1899, only three individuals were identified in the directories as real estate agents. They were P. Heiminck and Co., Isaac Cowie, and T. A. Stephen. Philip Heiminck was the Edmonton agent for the Hudson's Bay Co. and Cowie was the agent for the Scottish, Ontario, and Manitoba Land Co. Stephen is listed in the directory without any company affiliation.

By 1900 private land ownership had become an established institution in Edmonton with the creation of a Land Titles office. There was an oversupply of subdivided land on both sides of the river because the expected growth in population did not materialise. Selling real estate, therefore, employed just a few people. Events after 1900 would, however, dramatically improve Edmonton's prospects, as the second wave of transcontinental railway construction and the increased pace of land settlement would bring a decade of spectacular growth — when Edmonton would become one of western Canada's larger metropolitan areas.

Edmonton real estate agent Philip Heiminck was the Edmonton land agent for the Hudson's Bay Co.
(Provincial Archives of Alberta, B 8043)

The first ferry that crossed the North Saskatchewan River at Edmonton was established by John Walter and was located west of where the 105th street bridge is today.
(Provincial Archives of Alberta, A 3004)

CHAPTER TWO

Real Estate and the Railway Boom 1900-1913

The 1882 boom in Edmonton real estate caused by the anticipated arrival of the CPR gave Edmontonians a glimpse of the future.

During this period Edmontonians switched from protecting their claims to land speculation, as the construction of two transcontinental railways served as the basis for other investments. The excesses of this period, however, would give the real estate industry a reputation for dishonesty that would take years to overcome.

The railway boom of 1903 to 1913 was like the 1882 boom only it lasted longer and brought more permanent benefits to the city.

Organized real estate made a brief appearance in the form of the Edmonton Real Estate Exchange. While it had a minimal impact on the industry, it did introduce the idea of multiple listings and some administrative procedures that would be incorporated into future organizations. It was to

that extent the precursor of the present Edmonton Real Estate Board. Some of the Exchange's members continued to be active in later associations. This personal link with the past would be maintained by individuals such as H. Milton Martin and H. M. E. Evans.

While the evils of land speculation were widely debated, the government was slow in dealing with the problem. The attempts to control land speculation were minimal and were introduced only after the collapse of the boom.

Jasper Avenue (looking west from 99th Street) in 1903 shows how the streets of Edmonton had not yet been paved. Its commercial buildings were one- and two-storey brick and wood frame structures.
(Provincial Archives of Alberta, B 4768)

Railway construction

Before 1900, railways spurred on economic activity in Edmonton even when they did not actually arrive. In October 1902, the Edmonton, Yukon and Pacific Railway became the first railway to come to the incorporated town of Edmonton.

Jasper Avenue (looking west from 99th Street) in 1914 shows the physical transformation of Edmonton by the railway boom. Paved streets and a street railway system were two of the additions.
(Provincial Archives of Alberta, B 4852)

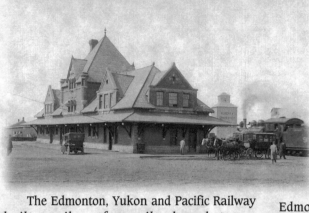

The Edmonton, Yukon and Pacific Railway built a railway four miles long between Edmonton and Strathcona using the Low Level Bridge, which had been built as a public work by the Federal Government.

The problem of providing Edmonton with a railway that had preoccupied it since the 1880s was finally resolved. No western Canadian community could survive — let alone prosper — if it did not have a railway. This railway connection was only a branch line, however, and being a terminal on the mainline of a railway was the key to substantial economic growth.

In 1903 Edmonton began to emerge as a national city when Canada's second generation of transcontinental railways began. Railway construction was the leading edge of private and public investment that transformed a town of 8,350 people covering an area of 3.4 square miles into a city of 72,516 people covering an area of 40.8 square miles by 1914.

Canadian Northern Railway

The first railway to begin land negotiations for a terminal with the Town of Edmonton was the Canadian Northern Railway Co. in 1902. By February, the Hudson's Bay Co. agreed to sell 68.88 acres of its Reserve to the City of Edmonton for $25,000 for use by the Canadian Northern. The Hudson's Bay Co. and the Canadian Northern each agreed to contribute $5,000 towards the purchase price. On March 5, 1903, Edmonton's businessmen raised the remaining $15,000. This amount was later repaid to the group with the passage of Bylaw 237. It raised $30,000 for

the purpose of granting the bonus to the Canadian Northern Railway and exempting it from taxation.

The land acquired by the Canadian Northern Railway in this transaction is now being redeveloped. A portion is occupied by Grant MacEwan Community College.

Grand Trunk Pacific Railway

The negotiations between the City of Edmonton, the Grand Trunk Pacific and the Canadian Pacific were far more complex. In 1903 Charles Melville Hays approached Edmonton City Council for an expression of support for the proposed railway. The resolution passed in response to this request stated that: "*Whereas the Edmonton District is rich in deposits of coal, timber and other natural resources which at the present time remain undeveloped and settlement eastward has already proceeded one hundred miles in anticipation of a throughline of railway, whilst settlement of the equally fertile land to the West is so much spoken of as to confidently warrant the assertion that it will be equally rapid and extensive as soon as railway facilities are in sight.*"

After the Grand Trunk Pacific Railway was incorporated, it asked the City of Edmonton to

buy land bounded by MacKenzie Avenue (104th) on the north; First Street (101st) on the east; Athabasca Avenue (102nd) on the south and Block sixteen of the Hudson's Bay Co. Reserve to the west.

In November 1904 the city began to obtain options on land for the proposed terminal. This land acquisition program, however, ran into problems when a number of owners refused to cooperate. As a consequence of the difficulties in acquiring land, the Council gave up on the idea of buying land and decided on a cash grant instead. In 1905, Council agreed to pay the Grand Trunk Pacific Railway $100,000. It also allowed the company to follow a right-of-way into the city that the Canadian Northern also intended to use. The Grand Trunk Pacific Railway was allowed to build tracks south of MacKenzie Avenue and was exempted from municipal taxation for five years. The company then purchased the land where Calder Yards are now located, north of the Hudson's Bay Co. Reserve.

that showed a crossing at 109th Street. By November 14, 1906, a tentative agreement was reached. It suggested turning part of Peace (103rd) and Athabasca (102nd) avenues into the railway yards, building railway bridges over Jasper and Saskatchewan avenues and highway bridges on Victoria (100th), McKay (99th), and Hardisty (98th) avenues. The City of Edmonton agreed to pay for the traffic portion of the High Level Bridge. Unlike the Low Level Bridge, the High Level went from top of the river bank to top of the river bank.

The High Level Bridge was intended to be a multipurpose structure which could be used by the Canadian Pacific, the street railway, pedestrians, and automobiles.

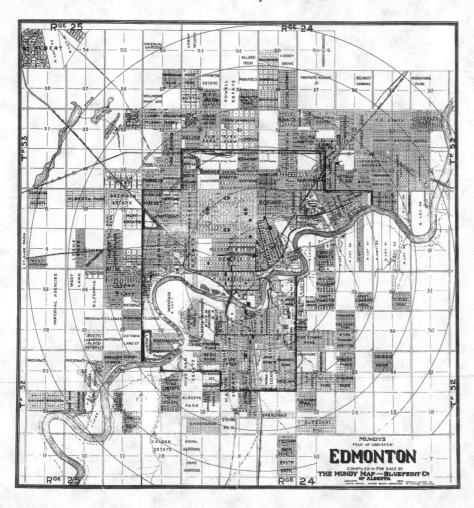

A map of Edmonton produced in 1912 by the Mundy Company shows the many new speculative subdivisions created during the railway boom.
(City of Edmonton Archives, EAM 31)

The Grand Trunk Pacific Railway also built what was then the most important commercial structure in Edmonton, the Hotel Macdonald.

In 1905, the Canadian Pacific Railway expressed interest in building into the City of Edmonton. In May of that year it filed plans

Edmonton's second real estate boom

Negotiations with railway companies rekindled the speculative spirit of 1881-1882. Investment in Edmonton real estate increased rapidly, as did the number of land promoters, real estate brokerage companies, and new subdivisions.

Between 1903 and 1914, 274 new subdivisions were created, which inflated the assessed value of city property to $191 million. Most of these existed only on paper and would never be developed. This rate represented an 1800 percent increase in the number of subdivisions on the north side alone compared with an 800 percent increase in the total population of Edmonton between 1904 and 1914.

These new subdivisions were located on both sides of the river, with the largest concentration being northeast of the central business district. Mundy's 1912 map of Greater Edmonton shows new subdivisions established as far as seven miles from the downtown area. The names chosen were common to other Canadian cities, and included Tuxedo Park and Queen Mary Park. With the exception of Windsor Park, Glenora, and Beau Park, these subdivisions did not deviate much from the grid pattern. The cumulative result was the creation of a blueprint for a "Greater Edmonton" that dazzled the imagination of Edmonton's boosters, strongly influenced many aspects of civic policy, and created new opportunities for Edmonton real estate brokerage firms.

The economic opportunities created by this boom led to the reorganization of some of Edmonton's pioneer firms, the best example being McDougall and Secord. On March 16, 1909, they formed McDougall and Secord Ltd. They dealt in a wide variety of investments, including stocks and bonds, and real estate for speculation and development. The firm also dealt in fire, life, and accident insurance and served as private bankers. They loaned mortgage money, created and administered trust funds, advanced money to other entrepreneurs, dealt in bills of exchange, promissory notes, coupons, drafts, debentures, and scrip, and bought and sold bullion.

Expansion of the industry

The boom in real estate attracted many new people who joined Edmonton's growing number of real estate and insurance agents, investment dealers, and land company representatives. The members of Edmonton's business community identified as real estate agents or as having any association with land companies went from 3 in 1899 to a peak of 333 in 1914.

Henry Marshall Erskin Evans was a member of this group of recently arrived businessmen who would help develop the city.

Evans was born at Davenport, Ontario, in 1876. He was a graduate of the University of Toronto and the School of Mines in Houghton, Michigan, where he had taken an assaying course. Evans had a varied business career before he moved to Edmonton. He spent some time in Mexico assisting in the administration of his uncle's mining interests. He came west in 1900 where he worked as business manager for the *Winnipeg Tribune*.

In 1905 he began his career in real estate by working for the Manitoba Land and Investment Co. This company was started by a group of American bankers who specialized in buying farming land and bringing in American settlers. Following Evans' departure from the land company, he came to Edmonton as the representative of John E. Burchard of St. Paul in order to test the extent of the coal deposits in what became the Evansburg area. His findings eventually led to the development of the town of Evansburg.

Evans moved permanently to Edmonton in 1907. He opened an office in the old Empire Block to sell real estate and insurance. He also served as a member of the

Henry Marshall Erskin Evans
(City of Edmonton Archives, EA-10-1532)

Interior of Western Realty Company as it was in 1909. This company was located on Jasper Avenue between 102 and 103 streets.
(City of Edmonton Archives, EA-10-2040)

local advisory committee and inspector of loans for the Northern Alberta Royal Trust Co., and was an inspector for the Mortgage Co. of Canada.

In 1910 he was appointed the Canadian agent for the Canadian Agency, an investment company based in London, England. Evans' experience made him an ideal choice, since this company wanted to invest British capital into the expanding economy of western Canada. Evans was proud of his association with the Canadian Agency in representing British capital.

The Canadian Agency was an investment company with various business interests in Canada, particularly in western Canada. Their Alberta companies included the Western Canada Land Co. This company owned 500,000 acres of land west and east of Edmonton, purchased from the Canadian Pacific Railway in 1905. It was a typical land company of the settlement period, having purchased the land in anticipation of rising land values.

Evans was also responsible for the Western Mortgage Co., Pembina Coal Co., Peace River Trading and Land Co., and Western Home Builders. Evans, like other real estate agents of his day, had to be active in other lines of business given the unpredictable market.

H. Milton Martin was another new arrival during this period. He moved to Edmonton in 1907 where he established the Crown Real Estate Co. in partnership with J. Almon Valiquette. In 1908 he established a firm under his own name.

He was born at Clintonville, New York, in 1872 but moved with his family at an early age, receiving his education in Quebec. He arrived in British Columbia in 1888 where he worked as a clerk, bookkeeper, and accountant for various companies. In 1898 he entered government service in the Yukon, rising to the position of Crown Timber and Land Agent for all of the Territory.

Martin's community involvement included serving as vice-president of the Edmonton Board of Trade in 1911 and as president of the Greater Edmonton Board of Trade in 1912. He was also a trustee on the Separate School Board and in charge of the financial affairs of the diocese of Edmonton.

Lou A. Weber arrived in 1911. According to an article in the August 3, 1911, *Daily Capital*, Lou Weber, formerly of Toronto, had spent the past month on an extensive tour through the Canadian west and had decided to make Edmonton his home. By August 1911 he had already leased a suite of offices in the new CPR building for his real estate business. Weber later added an insurance and loans branch. Lou Weber was formerly connected with the old and established real estate and insurance firm known as the ISK Weber Co. Ltd., with its head office at Kitchener, Ontario.

The influx of new businessmen also included Ed Molstad, a native of Rushford, Minnesota, who came to Edmonton in 1911. He was president and manager of the Fort George and Fraser Valley Land Co. His brother, John, who lived in Calgary, was vice-president and secretary-treasurer of the same company.

H. Milton Martin
(City of Edmonton Archives, EA-362-26)

New districts

The Highlands was a new district that began during this period. The community was developed by Magrath, Holgate and Co. W. J. Magrath arrived in Edmonton in 1904 from Belleville, Ontario, where he had operated a

cheese business. He soon entered the real estate business after creating Magrath, Hart and Co. This company was reorganized in 1909 when B.A. Holgate bought out Hart's interests. At first the company followed the traditional approach of simply creating subdivisions without proceeding with development.

Edmonton's new Street Railway is shown near residences at the corner of Jasper Avenue and 121 Street.
(Provincial Archives of Alberta, B 5006)

By 1910, 115th Street was a well established residential neighbourhood complete with boulevards and trees.
(Provincial Archives of Alberta, B 5004)

Subdivisions of this type created by this company included Bellevue in river lot twenty-eight, the Bellevue addition in river lot thirty, and Victoria Place and City Park, which were located immediately to the north.

They took a different approach with the Highlands subdivision, which was located on lots thirty-two and thirty-four. A promotional campaign began in September 1910 when Magrath, Holgate and Co. advertised that $50 in gold would be given to the person who provided the name for the new subdivision. In November 1911, building permits for twenty-eight private residences were taken out by the company. Included in this list were residences for Magrath and Holgate themselves.

Magrath, Holgate and Co. also negotiated with the city to provide various services to the district. In August 1911, the firm requested the extension of the street railway to the Highlands. The company agreed to bear the entire cost of the line from Borden Park, provided that it was constructed that fall and an hourly service was maintained. The company agreed to protect the Street Railway Department against loss for a period of eighteen months from the date the proposed line began operation. The company also negotiated an agreement to have certain streets paved in the subdivision.

The boom did not last long enough for the company to complete the development of the Highlands. The Holgate and Magrath mansions have survived, however, as reminders of their initial objectives. The construction of more modest homes continued into the post-World War Two period when the development of the district was completed.

Another company organized to develop residential property in Edmonton was Carruthers, Round and Co., which began in 1905. It was concerned with the creation of an exclusive district in the west end. James Carruthers, principal owner of the company, was a Montreal-based grain merchant who had extensive real estate investments in western Canada. Henry Round, who worked as the local agent for the company, was a former employee of the Hudson's Bay Co. He first came to Edmonton in 1884. The development of the Glenora subdivision began in 1906 when Carruthers purchased river lot two from Malcolm Groat. He subdivided the northern portion of the lot into a standard grid pattern. The land closer to the river, however, was surveyed to create curved streets to accommodate the ravines. Carruthers also negotiated an agreement with the City of Edmonton for the construction of a bridge across Groat Ravine and an agreement with the Province of Alberta to provide a site for the lieutenant governor's residence.

Carruthers also placed a restrictive covenant on all property in this area. It controlled the type, size, and number of buildings that could be built on each lot.

Calder was more of a working-class district developed in northwest Edmonton. In July 1910 the village of West Edmonton or Calder was established. West Edmonton was a company town for the Grand Trunk Pacific Railway. The Village of West Edmonton was annexed to the City of Edmonton in 1917.

The development of Calder is linked to the construction of the Grand Trunk Pacific Railway and the approach taken by the Hudson's Bay Co. to develop its Reserve. The HBC delayed the sale of that portion of its Reserve extending north from 107 Avenue until 1912. This decision forced the Grand Trunk Pacific Railway to locate its yards north of 122 Avenue. The result of the HBC's decision was the subdivision of the vacant land located north of the Hudson's Bay Co. Reserve.

The Magrath Mansion was built on Ada Boulevard in the Highlands in 1914. It was built for W. J. Magrath, whose firm was developing this subdivision.
(City of Edmonton Archives, EA-267-143)

Cloverdale was one of four river valley communities that was developed before World War One. Settlement began as early as the 1870s. By 1915 the neighbourhood was fully developed with schools, stores, local industries, and churches. Companies manufacturing forest products and bricks tended to locate in the valley.

A flood in 1915 eliminated the industries in these river valley communities.

Land speculation

The real estate boom rekindled land speculation, which had declined since 1881 when the first subdivision of land on the Hudson's Bay Co. Reserve occurred. Visitors to the City of Edmonton such as Wilhelm Cohnstaedt, who was in the city in 1909, reported that it was impossible to sit in a hotel lobby for more than five minutes without someone offering to sell land. His experience in the west led him to the conclusion that *a country in the process of settlement is overrun by real estate agents and land speculators.* In 1911, J. Burgon Bickersteth, a lay Anglican missionary in Edmonton, also marvelled at everyone's preoccupation with real estate.

Most of the land subdivision promoters were individuals and companies who were solely interested in creating a subdivision for immediate sale without any interest in actual development of the land. They were content to merely print advertisements extolling the beauty and investment potential of their respective subdivisions.

Stories about western Canadian land speculation appeared in newspapers such as *The Economist* of London, England, and the *Toronto Saturday Night.* The latter was particularly aggressive in its efforts to sort out legitimate investments from the frauds promoted by the "land sharks." The December 23, 1911, issue deals specifically with Edmonton in an article entitled "Fleecing the Credulous Land Buyer." It includes a detailed description of one method used. According to the article, real estate firms in Edmonton and in other western cities employed professional "cappers" from New York, to gather in "suckers" to buy their land. The plan involved placing an attractive painting of a subdivision in the window of a real estate office. Passersby

who stopped to admire it were engaged in conversation by the "cappers." The victims were induced to enter the office and invited to see the property offered for sale at the company's expense and in the company's automobile.

If the prospective buyer appeared sceptical about the value of the land, the "capper" would go along on the trip to the subdivision posing

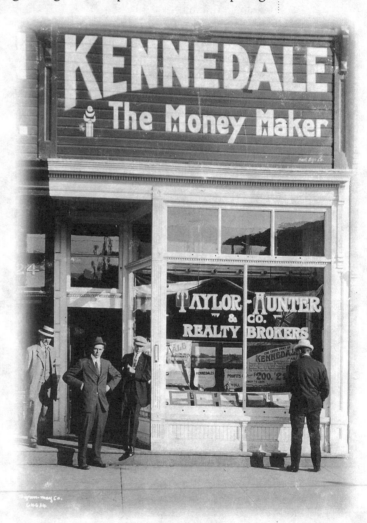

as a buyer. When they arrived at the property, the "capper" assumed the role of an experienced buyer who had seen real estate propositions in every town in the west, but had never seen any to equal this one. He would finally select two or three lots for himself while declaring he had not intended to buy when he left the office. With this example before him, the investor would be convinced that the property must be a safe deal.

The speculators bought lands adjacent to the city limits (and thus evaded city taxes), divided these into subdivisions, and sold as

This picture shows the front of the real estate office of Taylor-Hunter and Company, which was one of many promoting speculative subdivisions on the outskirts of the City of Edmonton.
(Glenbow Archives, NA-1328-64634)

many as they could before the pre-World War One depression. In this way they forced the city to annex these areas. Because the lots were outside the city and were unserviced, and because Edmonton refused to extend utilities to them, the residents of these areas began to apply to the Alberta Government for permission to be incorporated as towns. Edmonton disapproved of the incorporation of such municipalities into the city until their population warranted it. The villages of North Edmonton and Calder and the subdivisions of Elm Park and City View were annexed in this way. The result was the rapid extension of Edmonton's boundaries, with the last extension of the era being made in 1917 with the annexation of the Village of Calder. By 1914 the total area of the city was 40.8 square miles (105.7 square km) but the developed area was only 5.5 square miles (14.3 square km), representing 13.4 percent of the area of the city.

Promotion of the Highlands subdivision by Magrath-Holgate. The cars at the front of the real estate office were used to take prospective purchasers out to the site.
(City of Edmonton Archives, EA-160-489)

1911. Interested delegates were advised that *"every one in Edmonton who can possibly do so is investing in lots. It is in this way that those who have made fortunes have won the major portion of their wealth."*

People who had already purchased land in the subdivision were encouraged to sell it at a profit and buy more. As the company explained to one owner, *"our business is buying and selling real estate, and as this is the way in which people generally make their money on land investment, we are going to ask you to co-operate with us so that we may all make money . . . Thus,"* the letter concluded, *"the pot will be kept a-boiling."*

Radial Realty Co.

One company that dealt in these premature subdivisions was the Radial Realty Co., Ltd. Its name came from the Edmonton Interurban Railway between St. Albert and Edmonton whose land it controlled. It dealt in a variety of land investments, including city and suburban land, farm lands, coal areas, and timber limits. Its suburban properties included the subdivisions of Summerland, Radial Park, and Queen Mary Park, which were located between St. Albert and Edmonton.

The company's efforts to promote Queen Mary Park included letters to delegates at a teachers' convention in Edmonton in April

Hudson's Bay Co. land sale

The most celebrated example of land speculation was the Hudson's Bay Co. land sale in May 1912. The Hudson's Bay Co., which began the land boom tradition in Edmonton, had waited until May 13, 1912, to put most of its land on the market. The time for the sale was set at 2:00 p.m., but it did not announce the location. The location was discovered, however, by F.T. Aitken who installed himself at the door of the Little Gospel Mission Hall along with 2,000 other people. During the morning of May 13 numbered slips were given to those people who had waited through the night. This protected their place in the line but not the order in which they would be allowed to buy land. When the sale began, those with numbered slips were required to draw another ticket to determine the order in which they would be allowed to buy land.

Edmonton Real Estate Exchange

The Edmonton real estate business community was concerned about the problem of subdivisions outside Edmonton's boundaries since they had the potential to destroy the confidence of outside investors in the Edmonton land market. They reacted to the land speculation by organizing the Edmonton Real Estate Exchange in June of 1909. It was formed, according to reports in the press, to bring the real estate men of Edmonton together to help advance the interests of the city at large and of the real estate business in particular. They decided to implement a uniform rate of commission, create and maintain among Edmonton real estate men a high standard of integrity, and encourage a spirit of fair and honourable competition. The result of this approach would be: "*securing to the buyer and seller the services of responsible and trustworthy agents upon a definite and uniform standard of contract and charges, to the end that the interests of the buyer, seller and broker may be alike protected.*"

The Edmonton Real Estate Exchange also began Edmonton's first multiple listing service. Only twenty-three companies were members of the Exchange and thus it represented only a small percentage of the companies operating in Edmonton at that time. Owners could list their property with one agent who would then share this listing with other members of the Exchange. Such an approach, according to this same article, avoided the trouble and inconvenience of answering many enquiries and notifying many agents of changes in price or terms. Prospective purchasers would benefit because members of the Exchange would have the widest choice of available properties.

The Exchange was run by an executive made up of a president, a vice-president, a secretary-treasurer, and five directors. Standing committees were also formed to help the Exchange. They were called Legislation and Publicity; Finance; Membership and References; Valuation and Arbitration; and Commission.

People lined up on May 13, 1912, to purchase lots in the Hudson's Bay Company Co. Reserve.
(City of Edmonton Archives, EA-157-412)

Land shows

The Edmonton Chamber of Commerce also tried to deal with the problem of land speculation. They thought that legislation could protect the legitimate investor and stop property advertisements that failed to show the whole of the town or city in or near the property's location. At a council meeting in December 1911, the real estate section agreed to ask for this legislation. *Toronto Saturday Night* enthusiastically endorsed the proposal.

The Chamber of Commerce took more direct action against speculators when a land show and home building exhibit was being planned. At their meeting on March 12, 1912, the Chamber of Commerce passed a motion to disassociate itself from this event. H. Milton Martin, chairman of the meeting, reported that the Board of Trade had obtained information on the show from businessmen in Calgary before taking this position. One of the telegrams received indicated that "*it was a money making scheme and did not by any means come up to the standards it was boosted to be.*"

When a similar show was planned for November 1912, the real estate section of the Board of Trade tried unsuccessfully to prevent it. The show was held on November 16, 1912, at the Thistle Rink. The *Edmonton Bulletin* observed in its November 20, 1912, issue that the show was: *"proving to be a great boon to the local real estate men who are numbered among the exhibitors. Their booths are all elaborately fitted up and a staff of salesmen are on hand to cater to prospective buyers."*

The *Edmonton Journal* articles on the fair also confirmed public interest

A few months ago when things seemed rather quiet along the real estate rialto, some dealers predicted that the early winter would witness a remarkable revival in city and district property. The pessimist said it was "hot air" or something to that effect. But the pessimist as is usually the case was entirely wrong. The activity "boom," some people call it has arrived and it promises to be one of the biggest in the history of the city.

The Edmonton and western Canadian real estate market by 1912 had become a giant selling scheme on the verge of collapse. Its decline began in June 1913.

This pre-World War boom era is important to the history of the Edmonton Real Estate Board because it shows the first attempt to establish organized real estate. The Edmonton Real Estate Exchange was an early form of multiple listing bureau in which companies cooperated in the sharing of listings. It also endeavoured to promote a high standard of business ethics at a time when land speculation was rampant. The organization of the Exchange would also establish the importance of standing committees. All of these features would be incorporated into the way later organizations would operate through to the present day.

Various real estate schemes left a generally negative public image of the industry. This negative reputation would take years to eliminate.

The railway boom had expanded the city in population and physical size. Edmonton became the capital of the new Province of Alberta and one of the five major urban centres in western Canada. The extra land incorporated into the city because of land speculation would also eliminate the need for further annexations until after World War Two.

CHAPTER THREE

War and Depression
1914-1939

The collapse of the western Canadian real estate market in 1913 was unexpected, at least to the boosters, and severe. It did, however, stop large scale land speculation for a while. A vast amount of subdivided land on the fringes of Edmonton remained undeveloped.

The Hudson's Bay Co. Reserve, which had been the cause of such excitement in 1912, also remained undeveloped until Blatchford Field was established, now known as The Edmonton Municipal Airport.

During the recession, the real estate community throughout Alberta came to realize the need for some form of regulation for their members. In 1927, members of the real estate industry of Edmonton established the Edmonton Real Estate Association. This organization struggled for years to survive but it kept alive the idea of organized real estate. It was responsible for the passage of the first act to regulate the industry. Modifications to that act in future years and cooperation between the government and industry as a result of its passage brought substantial benefits to the whole industry and to the general public.

Recession

From 1900 to 1912, unprecedented levels of public and private investment financed Edmonton's expansion as a transportation, industrial, and commercial centre. Many people moving to Edmonton also contributed to its growth. The recession of 1913 and World War One, however, brought an end to this flow of investment and immigration and thus an end to Edmonton's boom town psychology. Edmonton suffered when financial, human, and material resources were taken from frontier development and put towards the war effort because few war-related industries were developed in Edmonton.

Boosterism was replaced with patriotism as future expansion was deferred in the interest of winning the war.

Collapse of the land boom

World War One marked a basic and inevitable adjustment in Edmonton's economy unrelated to the events in Europe. This change was noted by H. M. E. Evans, the chairman of the recently established Edmonton Board of Public Welfare, in his first annual report. The economic expansion, he noted: *"could not last and (it) showed unmistakable signs of passing even before the outbreak of the War. Therefore, while the sudden collapse in the autumn of 1914 forced the matter urgently on our attention and the operations of the Board for that year were mainly in the nature of emergency relief measures, the problem was inevitable and will be permanent."*

The collapse of the urban real estate market left an oversupply of land available for development. This problem was not solved by the war or the postwar recovery during the late 1920s. From 1920 to 1938, the city laid out on paper during the boom was dismantled.

This meant many subdivisions such as Mayfair Park (where Hawrelak Park is now) were cancelled. Plans for the development of a civic centre were also abandoned.

Downtown Edmonton is shown in 1929. The Hotel Macdonald was the most prominent site on the Edmonton skyline from 1916 to the 1960s.
(City of Edmonton Archives, EA-64-2)

The legacy of the pre-World War One railway boom was that Edmonton was now a city covering 40.8 square miles (105.67 square km) or 26,342 acres (10,668.51 hectares) of which only 4,730 acres (1,915.65 hectares) or 18 percent was serviced with water and sewer lines. The city was committed through annexation agreements to extend water and sewer services to much of the undeveloped land in the suburban zones. The suburban zones, although divided into blocks and lots, were basically agricultural land. Yet its assessed value before 1921 was inflated from an average of $100 per acre ($250 per hectare), which would have been reasonable, to $274 per acre ($685 per hectare). Because of the financial stringency of the time, it became very difficult to collect the taxes that were levied on the lots in this area. By September 1915 the solvency of the city was threatened. The city responded with a massive tax sale of much of this property.

One obvious effect was the drastic drop in the number of real estate firms listed in the *Henderson's Directory,* which went from a peak of 333 in 1914, to 101 in 1920. The Radial Realty Co., whose reason for being had been the promotion of the outside subdivisions, did not survive.

Lou Weber's company survived by diversifying into insurance. He was joined by his brother N. Roy Weber in 1915 to establish Weber Brothers. N. Roy Weber had originally come west in 1911 but had settled in Calgary where he was employed by the Winnipeg-based Walch Land Co. He rose to become manager and then exclusive agent of this company before it went out of business during

The Garneau district shown here in 1930 was established during the pre-World War One boom.
(City of Edmonton Archives, EA-10-159)

the First World War. The partnership between Lou and Roy proved to be very successful, with Roy being primarily concerned with real estate while Lou handled the insurance side. The company dealt in fire insurance at first but branched out into other lines, particularly automobile insurance.

In 1923 the brothers incorporated the first automobile finance company in the province, the Edmonton Credit Co.

Other brokers, such as Ed Molstad who had been involved with the Fort George Land Co., also switched to other endeavours such as insurance. In 1916, Molstad became branch manager of Excelsior Life Insurance Co. and later became district superintendent.

H. M. E. Evans had other problems in addition to the decline in investment and the drop in the real estate market. On June 10, 1914, the Canadian Agency failed. Evans was able to acquire the stock of the Western Canada Mortgage Co. and the Western Homebuildings Ltd. upon which he built new companies, including H. M. E. Evans and Co., Homevans Investment Ltd., and British Alberta Investments Ltd. In addition to reconstructing his own business career, he played an active role in civic affairs to help Edmontonians cope with the end of the boom.

Economic expansion in the late 1920s

The recession that began in 1913 and continued after World War One ended in the mid-1920s. Settlement of the Peace River Country resumed and an oil boom temporarily rekindled the expectations of the pre-World War One era. The oil boom in Alberta was stimulated by developments in the Turner Valley oil field and in the Wainwright area.

According to prosperity advertisements in various western newspapers, land purchases and immigration to the Prairies in 1928 were far ahead of anything since pre-war days. Unemployment had given way to actual labour shortages.

The prosperity of the late 1920s did not result in the same type of land speculation as before. Even so, the *Edmonton Journal* in a March 29, 1928, article did see a glimmer of hope for a return to boom times.

An important addition to the central business district during the interwar period was the new Canadian National Railways station, which opened on March 17, 1928.
(City of Edmonton Archives, B 6102)

Boom times were somewhat approached on Tuesday morning when numerous sales of city lots were approved by the commissioners. The morning's transfers proved to be the heaviest in point of numbers that the city has handled for some time.

Chief among the deals was the sale of a lot at 101 Street and 106 Avenue to a gasoline supply company for $3,600 cash.

Under another deal which involved the sale of four city lots at 97 Street and 115 Avenue in Norwood, there was a yield of $1,300 cash. The purchaser has agreed to proceed with the erection of four modern bungalows, each costing $3,000 on this property.

The city has also sold a lot at 88 Street and 117 Avenue in Norwood for $225 cash, while a building in the Rutherford addition brought $100 cash. Three lots in Forest Heights were sold for $100.

The sale of city land virtually came to a halt. The City of Edmonton continued to be the major land owner until after World War Two.

The increased sale of city land during the late 1920s was no portent of future events. On October 29, 1929, the New York Stock Exchange crashed, followed by the Canadian stock market crash. The Great Depression had begun. The news of the crash in New York did not have an immediate effect on the Edmonton real estate market. On January 18, 1930, it was reported that: *"the first big real estate deal in Edmonton city property this year and the first for some time was consummated Friday afternoon when the Fairburn Apartments were purchased for $60,000."* By the end of January 1930, though, drastic drops in wheat prices were being reported in Winnipeg. Between January 1930 and January 1931 the price of Number 1 Northern Wheat fell from $1.11 to 34 cents per bushel. Effects of the Depression on real estate lasted until the beginning of World War Two.

The Birks Building on Jasper Avenue and 104th Street was constructed at the end of the 1920s.
(Edmonton Real Estate Board)

Creation of the Edmonton Real Estate Association

The economic upsurge of the late 1920s lasted long enough for the real estate industry in Edmonton to re-establish an association. On September 25, 1926, a meeting organized by J. D. O. Mothersill, an Edmonton lawyer, and John McIntosh, land agent for the Hudson's Bay Co., was held at the Chamber of Commerce. They discussed the idea of organizing an Edmonton real estate exchange. Andy Whyte, Percy Barager, Jack Bagley, Frank Lorimer, Elmer Pointer, George Gowan, and John Brown also attended. These men represented Whyte and Co.; Bessey, Bagley and McNanus; Chauvin, Allsopp and Co.; and the General Administration Society.

The men looked at the Vancouver Real Estate Exchange as a model for this new organization. George Gowan provided information on it and circulated a copy of its constitution and bylaws. As noted in Anne Broadfoot's book (published in 1995), *Real Estate Board of Greater Vancouver, A History of Service, 1919 / 1994*, its members were

committed to high standards of practice and to advance the interests of the City of Vancouver and greater Vancouver area and its citizens by collection and circulation of valuable and useful information pertaining to the purchase, maintenance and sale of real property.

Members also agreed to oppose enactments of laws detrimental to real estate ownership. They guaranteed to subscribe funds for education to upgrade the industry, to adopt and enforce sound rules of business conduct among those engaged in real estate and to develop a strict code of ethics for the protection of the consumer of real estate services.

A committee was created to investigate the matter further. They presented a report on February 14, 1927, that suggested another form that organized real estate could take. The choice was between forming a new exchange affiliated with the National Real Estate Board, or reviving the Alberta Real Estate Association, whose present officers were residents of Calgary. (The jurisdiction of the new association was to be limited to the territory north of Red Deer.) Another committee was created to resolve the issue of how the Edmonton real estate industry should organize.

The second committee presented their report on February 28, 1927. It advised against forming a real estate exchange because of the difficulty financing its operations and because few Edmonton real estate agents would have the time to devote to making it a success. Those present agreed with these conclusions.

As an alternative to creating an exchange, the committee recommended creating a special committee to speak to Cabinet about applying for legislation on the licensing of real estate

agents. It was also recommended that representatives from Calgary, Lethbridge, Medicine Hat, and other communities be invited to work with the local committee to bring about the passage of this legislation.

After the committee presented its report, an ad hoc legislative committee was appointed to interview the government, and Andy Whyte was delegated to interview officials of the Alberta Real Estate Association about their opinions on this matter.

On March 15, 1927, Jack Bagley reported on the favourable reception the legislative committee had received from Attorney General John Lymburn. Given this success, the committee drafted an act for presentation to the House and hired Joseph Mothersill, of Mothersill and Dyde, to help them prepare the proposed bill. The expenses were to be covered by the Alberta Real Estate Association or by Edmonton real estate agents up to a maximum of $200.

The initial success of this committee led to the creation of the Edmonton Real Estate Association. After Jack Bagley, chairman of the Legislation Committee, made his report he also moved that a local association be formed to be known as the Edmonton Real Estate Association. This motion was carried unanimously and work began immediately to bring this about.

On March 21, 1927, the nomination committee presented their report. Elected candidates were Frank Lorimer, Jack Bagley, and Emory Wood. Subsequent presidents through to 1939 included Frank Lorimer, John Joseph Duggan, H. Milton Martin, Ralph Blackmer, Robert H. Watson, N. Roy Weber, Luke Winterburn, John Killen, Sid Lawrie, and Sam Ferris.

When Frank Lorimer was elected president in 1927 he was the manager of the real estate department of Chauvin, Allsopp and Co. He held that position until 1932 when he went into a brief partnership with Robert Watson. In 1933 he established his own company. He served as president again in 1928 and in 1937.

Joseph Duggan was a native of Wales who had come to Edmonton in 1913. He became secretary-treasurer of the Duggan Building and Investment Co. In 1919 he went into partnership with his brother, Milwyn Duggan, and Ray Emmott to form the Duggan and Duggan Real Estate Co. In 1920 he established the J. J. Duggan Co. Ltd., which dealt in insurance investments, loans, and country real estate in the form of ranches and farms. The company was also the general agents for the United Grain Growers' Securities Co. Ltd. He was president of this company until he went into government service in 1935. The Duggan district in the southwest part of Edmonton is named after him. He served as president in 1929.

Joseph Duggan's record of community service began in 1917 when he was elected to the Edmonton Public School Board, where he served three years. He was a member of city council in 1924 and 1925. Joseph was a member of the Alberta Assessment Commission from 1927 to 1937. He was on the public library board from 1927 to 1933 with the exception of 1931.

H. Milton Martin had already established himself as a community leader before he became president of the Edmonton Real Estate Association in 1930, by serving as chairman of the Town Planning Commission.

Ralph Blackmer arrived in Edmonton in 1918. He was first employed as an accountant for the Western Canada Land Co. By 1924 he had become sales manager of the Western Canada Land Co. and secretary of H. M. E. Evans and Co., Ltd. In 1925 he was placed in charge of the Farm Lands Department of H. M. E. Evans and Co., a position he would hold until his death in 1945. He served as president in 1931.

Robert Watson was an inspector with the General Administration Society, a Montreal-based company which handled real estate as well as insurance. He was a partner in the firm of Lorimer and Watson during his term as president in 1932. After the end of this partnership he worked for Cowan and Co. and eventually moved to Brewster, Cross and Taylor, where he was an insurance adjuster.

N. Roy Weber (as described earlier) was one of the partners in the firm of Weber Brothers. He had joined his brother Lou, to establish the company in 1915. He was a two-term president serving in 1933 and 1934 when the Depression was at its worst in terms of unemployment.

Born in Manchester, England, on June 25, 1878, Luke Winterburn later attended school at Oldham, about seven miles (11 kilometres) from Manchester. He later set up his own firm, Winterburn Motor Haulage Contractors. It was the largest of its kind in Oldham at the time. Luke had five steam wagons, three furniture vans, and half a dozen horses. He recalled hauling a huge gas drum on a steam wagon, with an engine fired by coke, 190 miles (304 kilometres) at a speed of 5 miles (8 kilometres) per hour. The pay was less than $100.

Luke came to Alberta in 1912, settling first in Fort Macleod. He then went to work with a Dominion survey party in the Rockies for six months. In March 1913 he moved to Edmonton and went into business in the Old Gariepy Block. The name of his firm, taken over from S.

P. Wilson of W. W. Sales, was Northern Brokers. Two years later he joined forces with the Fletcher Realty Co., and some years later went into partnership with Hake to form the company Hake and Winterburn. It was located in the Bellamy Block. He subsequently moved to the Campbell Furniture Building and then to the Agency Building. He served as president in 1935. His business interest also included the development of the subdivisions of Woodland Addition, Balwin and Hawin.

Another arrival from the British Isles was John Killen who came to Edmonton in 1901 from Belfast, Ireland, with the intention of going on to Australia. Instead, he went into the real estate and insurance business with Henry Gilbert in 1902. He remained active in the industry until 1954 and was president of the Edmonton Real Estate Association in 1936.

After ten years in the Edmonton real estate business Sid Lawrie became president of the Board in 1938. In 1928 he had established Lawrie Investment Agencies, which dealt in farm and city property as well as rentals, insurance, loans, and bonds. He was able to survive the Depression by the age-old method of diversifying his services.

Sam Ferris came to Edmonton in 1906. He was born in Shelburne, Ontario. He was educated at Hornings Mills, Shelburne, and Owen Sound, Ontario, and apprenticed in the mercantile business in 1904. Upon his arrival in Edmonton he went to work for the City of Edmonton as a clerk in the electric light department. He became city cashier and pay master in the treasury department in 1910 and assistant city assessor from 1914 to 1918. Sam organized the City Land Department and was superintendent of that department from 1921 to 1928. He quit in 1928 to become manager of Weber Bros. Agencies Ltd., Real Estate Department until 1938, when he established his own firm. He became president of the Edmonton Real Estate Association the following year.

Other individuals who contributed to the Association's operations between 1927 and 1939 but did not serve as president at this time included Andy Whyte and Mark Cummings.

Andy Whyte arrived in Edmonton in 1925. Before that he lived in Moosomin, Saskatchewan, where he was mayor for several years. Born in Leeds, Quebec, in 1865, he worked in various stores until he gained the experience to start his own operations. In 1892 he branched out by starting a chain of stores in Manitoba and in what is now Saskatchewan.

A close associate of Andy Whyte's was Mark Cummings who was born in Virden, Manitoba, in 1901. His first job was in the Union Bank in Rosetown, Saskatchewan. He quit when he found out that his wages did not cover the cost of his frequent moves from one bank to another. He moved to Edmonton in 1932 where he purchased the Hamilton Flour and Feed mill. He established Cummings Agencies Ltd. in 1936 after selling the feed mill. In 1948 he established Western Canada Appraisal Ltd. in partnership with Andy Whyte. He served as president of the Edmonton Real Estate Association in 1947. Mark played a leading role in the establishment of the Alberta Real Estate Association (AREA) and was an active member of the Canadian Real Estate Association (CREA). He was made a Life Member of the EREB in recognition of these contributions.

Andy Whyte played a leading role in the creation of the Alberta Real Estate Association and the Canadian Real Estate Association.
(Edmonton Real Estate Board)

The first constitution

The drafting of a constitution was completed by April 1927. The National Association of Real Estate Boards' constitution was taken as a guide, with any articles and clauses not applicable to the operation of a real estate association in Edmonton being struck out.

The constitution of the new Association was a detailed document that dealt with objectives, membership, government, and ethics. It remained largely unchanged until the 1940s.

The first objective was: *"to unite the real estate men of this community for the purpose of exerting effectively a combined influence upon matters affecting real estate interests."*

The second objective was to encourage the adoption of rules and regulations to facilitate business transactions by its members.

The third objective was to promote and enforce high standards of conduct by its members based on the code of ethics.

A final objective was to advance the civic development and the economic growth of Edmonton.

Membership

Membership in the Association required the approval of the board of directors and the general membership. Members were divided into two general classes. The first was for owners or officers of a corporation engaged in the sale of real estate. The second class was for salesmen of those firms that were members of the Association.

In addition to these two classes of membership, the constitution also required all members to sign a personal pledge. Fines and expulsion from the Association would result if members did not comply with the bylaws or code of ethics, or for: *"any conduct which [tended] to cause discredit to fall upon the Association or upon the real estate business as a whole."*

The privileges and obligations of individual members included reporting to the board of directors in writing any breaches made by members. Such reports were *"deemed a privileged communication and [did] not subject the member making such a report to liability."* Upon the receipt of a complaint the board of directors was required to advise the member of the complaint, provide the member with a copy of the letter, and start an investigation.

Membership fees and dues were arranged according to the membership structure. The first member representing an office was required to pay $10. Each additional member of that firm including salesmen paid $5 each.

The owners or employees of companies that were members of the Association were responsible for the actions of that company unless they could show: *"to the satisfaction of the Board of Directors that such violation was without his or their knowledge or consent."*

The Association was governed by an eight-member board of directors. A nominating committee (appointed at least two weeks before the annual meeting) arranged elections of officers and directors. The officers were authorized to hire an executive secretary and any: *"such other persons as may be necessary to properly conduct the activities of the Association."*

The Association was not large or active enough to justify the hiring of a full-time executive secretary until the late 1950s.

At certain times the office of secretary and treasurer were combined. Secretarial duties were, therefore, handled by Association members who were paid a small honorarium for performing these tasks.

Standing committees

The constitution also established a system of standing committees that would help to achieve the Association's various objectives. The evolution of this system is a major part of the Edmonton Real Estate Board's administrative history from 1927 to 1995. The standing committees in 1927 were Appraisal; Arbitration; Membership; Program; Legislative; and Publicity. The only committee not carried forward from 1909 was Finance.

Helping members when problems arose in making an appraisal and reponding to requests to the Association for appraisals from an outside body was the responsibility of the Appraisal Committee.

Adjudicated complaints or differences between members was the responsibility of the Arbitration Committee. The committee only heard cases when the parties involved had agreed in writing to abide by its findings without recourse to any other tribunal, and to pay all costs of the proceedings. The

committee functioned in a semi-judicial fashion by obtaining statements under oath from the principals and witnesses. The secretary of the Association gave a written reply within forty-eight hours of the committee's decision. A copy was signed by the deciding members and the seal of the Board attached by the secretary. The committee was required to keep a record of each dispute, the decisions made, and the grounds for the decisions.

The task of building up the membership, maintaining the interest of the members, and having members attend all the meetings was the task of two committees, namely the Membership and Program committees. The Program Committee provided the programs for the meetings that were: *"for the best interest and welfare of the Association."* Publicizing the activities of the Association was the responsibility of another committee. The Publicity Committee also sought new members.

The Legislative Committee was to: *"guard and promote the interests of real estate before all legislative bodies whether civic or provincial. . . ."* This committee was thus responsible for reviewing new legislation and suggesting changes to existing statutes.

Code of Ethics

The constitution of the National Real Estate Association provided the code of ethics for the new association. Its comprehensive rules of conduct dealt with an individual broker's relationship with fellow brokers, clients, customers, and the public.

The Edmonton Real Estate Association was designed to do more than encourage integrity and full disclosure amongst members of the real estate industry. It encouraged the self-regulation of the industry, cooperation between brokers, efficient office practices, and education.

The Association in operation

By May 1927, the necessary steps had been taken to organize the Edmonton Real Estate Association. The first general meeting was held on May 16, 1927. Joseph Mothersill's presentation stressed the pitfalls of new organizations and a few of the things a real estate association might do. John Blue, secretary of the Edmonton Board of Trade, discussed the value of an organization among the members of any profession or business and also the need for immigrants to Alberta. Musical presentations were also part of the program.

The Membership, Program, Publicity, and Legislative committees were most active between 1927 and 1938. In June 1927, the Publicity Committee informed local newspapers of the proceedings of the Association. The *Edmonton Journal* and the *Edmonton Bulletin* showed no interest since virtually no press coverage of the Association's activities is evident before the 1950s.

In July 1928, the Association launched its first membership drive. Both Sid Lawrie and Luke Winterburn joined as a result of this effort. Their contributions would include serving as presidents of the Association.

The problems of decreasing membership and low attendance at the meetings became acute during the 1930s. Fees were dropped to as low as $1. In 1935 the Association considered joining the real estate section of the Chamber of Commerce. One reason suggested in support of the idea was that a delegation from the real estate section would have more impact on governments than the Edmonton Real Estate Association would. Frank Lorimer, however, objected to the way the Edmonton Chamber of Commerce was run. He said: *"that all they had done was to get a person's membership, arrange for a few speakers, invite the entire membership and that was practically all there was to do."*

The Real Estate Agents' Licensing Act

The Legislative Committee worked to bring about legislation on the licensing of real estate agents. Legislation relating to the industry before 1929 included "The Land Titles Act" and "The Real Estate Commission Act," both passed in 1906.

The first effort to bring in additional legislation was initiated by the Calgary Real Estate Board. In 1919 it proposed a law requiring real estate brokers to be licensed. To obtain this license, the names of ten residents

in the locality of the proposed business were required along with a bond and a license fee of $100. Ten dollars was charged for each salesman working under the license. According to Edmund Taylor, the legislation was needed because of the operations of unqualified or unscrupulous people who discredited the industry.

This initiative prompted a conference in Calgary on December 12, 1919, of real estate men in the province, including representatives from Edmonton. The meeting produced a number of revisions to meet the concerns of other real estate agents in the province. However, while there was strong support from the industry, no legislation came about.

By March 21, 1927, a draft copy of the legislation was approved for presentation to Premier Brownlee and Attorney General John Lymburn. The provincial government provided further encouragement when on June 6, 1927, Lymburn made a presentation to the Association. Henry Brace, the superintendent of insurance, also met with the Association to suggest revisions.

The draft bill was introduced into the Alberta Legislature on February 3 and debate began on February 16. The draft bill required all real estate agents to be bonded in the sum of $1,000. It also outlined a fee schedule based on the size of the town in which the transaction took place. The fee was $10 in towns and cities of 5,000 or more; $7.50 in towns or cities of less than 5,000, and $3 elsewhere in the province. The license fee for a real estate salesman was set at $3, and $1 was to be charged if the license had to be amended or reinstated.

Considerable opposition to the bill arose because trust companies and lawyers were exempt from paying the bond required from full-time real estate agents. Archie Matheson – the member for Vegreville – led the attack on this provision of the draft bill. He was supported by Gordon Foster, the member for Hand Hills, and P. Christophers, the member for Rocky Mountain House. Both appeared to have a deep-rooted antipathy towards the legal profession. Christophers expressed the view that *"while he was not familiar with lawyers he knew enough to keep out of their clutches."*

This criticism of lawyers brought Liberal leader Joe Shaw and Attorney General John Lymburn to their defence. Shaw pointed out that: *"no matter how much a limited number of lawyers may have erred in the past, that one swallow does not make a summer, and that lawyers breaking the law had no special privileges when they came before the law."* Attorney General John Lymburn also defended the business morality of lawyers, indicating that it was as high, if not higher, as in any other business, including farming.

Following the debate on the morality of lawyers, the House resumed its debate on the bill. In the end, trust companies could engage in the real estate business without payment of the bond but members of the law society were barred from business of this nature. Foster and Matheson also tried to change the amount of the bond from $1,000 to $5,000 and then to $2,000 but both amendments were defeated.

Further debate took place on March 19, when Lorne Proudfoot, the member from Acadia, raised other objections. His criticism, reported in the *Edmonton Bulletin*, was that

> *legislation of this type especially in rural districts where people were acquainted one with another, was superfluous. To the best of his knowledge there had been no demand for such legislation.*
>
> *If the government desired these fees for a source of revenue let that declaration be made without fear or favour. He thought this was not the best method of protecting people from being beaten out of their money.*
>
> *He submitted farmers might just as well be licensed so that they wouldn't put all the large potatoes on the top of the sack or water their milk. The whole trend of legislation of this type was becoming ridiculous. In addition it would work a hardship on the small man whose turn over was limited.*

Proudfoot's suggestion that bonding be reduced or eliminated altogether was favourably received. Passage of the bill thus became dependent on resolving the issue of bonding.

With the passage of the bill in jeopardy, the Edmonton Real Estate Association considered revisions to their original draft and intensified their lobbying efforts in support of this legislation in anticipation of its resubmission in 1929. On April 2, 1928, John MacIntosh suggested that a petition signed by a representative body of real estate men might

have some influence with them. Requesting support from local Boards of Trade was also suggested. In August the Edmonton Real Estate Association also launched a fund-raising effort. Edmonton and Calgary were expected to contribute $3,000 each, Lethbridge and Medicine Hat to contribute $100 each, and all other towns to contribute $50 each. It is not known if they reached their target.

Despite considerable support for keeping the bonding provisions and financial donations from such organizations as the Alberta Real Estate Association, the Edmonton Real Estate Association changed its views on the bonding issue. With the elimination of the bonding provision, the bill was passed in the 1929 sitting. It received royal assent by March 20.

This bill was significant because it was the first step by the government to require persons to furnish some assurance of their qualifications to act as real estate agents. The Real Estate Agents' Licensing Act included definitions of a real estate agent and a salesman, of a superintendent as a regulatory authority, as well as licensing requirements, grounds for suspension or cancellation, contravention, penalties, and fees.

After the passage of the bill, the Edmonton Real Estate Association continued to consider improvements. At the executive meeting on December 30, 1929, it was suggested that the Real Estate Act be amended to make it an offence to pay a commission to anyone other than a licensed agent and that all agents must furnish a bond. These and other suggestions were forwarded to the Legislative Committee for action.

The Edmonton Real Estate Association also worked closely with the administrator of the act, Henry Brace, to ensure its enforcement.

Matthew A. Hammond was one individual whose conduct concerned the Association. At the October 21, 1929, meeting, Messrs. Hake and Winterburn complained that he loitered outside their office and solicited their customers. It was decided that the president would interview Brace to see if there was any remedy against such tactics. The president later reported that an inspector had cautioned Hammond, who had promised not to repeat the offence. Brace also said that if Hammond could be convicted under any city bylaw Brace would not hesitate to cancel his license.

Other issues dealt with by special committees created by the Association through to 1939 included the development of a standardized commissions schedule and standardized forms. In the fall of 1927, work began on revising the interim contract form, standard listing form, and the offer-to-purchase form.

Community involvement

Town planning was a community issue of interest to the Association during 1927 to 1938. The Association continued work on comprehensive policies and on the development of specific areas in the city. In August 1927, for example, City Council asked the Association to be a member of a town planning and zoning committee. It consisted of aldermen and representatives from various public organizations who acted as advisors to the City Council on these issues.

When the Town Planning Commission was established in 1929 the Association played a more permanent role. The Commission was authorized to prepare a major street plan and a zoning bylaw, which was completed in 1933. H. Milton Martin served as chairman of the Commission during this period. The tradition of Board involvement on this Commission was carried on by Luke Winterburn. Sid Lawrie was the Board's representative on the Zoning Appeal Board.

The Association also became involved in the ongoing issue of Edmonton's civic centre development, which had been shelved because of the high land costs. At the October 17, 1927, meeting, Alderman Gibbs discussed the objectives of the Town Planning Committee and *"invited the fullest co-operation of the Association in their deliberation."* He also reviewed the history of the civic centre plans and showed maps on the proposed lay-out and the small amount of property to be acquired. After his presentation, a committee was appointed to interview those private land owners who were holding out for a price considered above its real value. These meetings — if they took place — had no effect on the civic centre development at that time.

In November 1929, John Yule, the Association's secretary, drew attention to the lack of street number signs and posts. In his letter to the city, John Yule noted that the

"absence of these signs, apart from being an inconvenience to the citizens gives the city a neglected appearance and causes strangers to form a bad impression."

By 1939, the effects of the Depression on the Edmonton real estate market were less evident. In his president's report for 1938-39, Sam Ferris reported that

there appears to be no doubt that the real estate market has greatly improved during the past year. Many more sales of house properties have been made, and there are indications of business properties becoming more active on the market. Rentals remain steady at practically the same standard of value that they were a year ago.

There is the same shortage of housing spaces as well as certain types of space for business purposes.

Ferris also noted with satisfaction that the present war had not injured the market. He also thought that people were *"becoming more real estate minded all the time, and are taking a renewed interest in this form of investment."*

The creation of the Edmonton Real Estate Association in 1927 established the two-tiered membership system, which would remain unchanged until 1995. The creation of this organization reflected the prosperity of the late 1920s. The Association initiated the first cooperation between the Edmonton real estate community and the provincial government. The Real Estate Agents' Licensing Act and its subsequent revisions provided the legislative framework for the industry until the passage of the Real Estate Act in 1995.

The high hopes of 1927 were tested during the Depression. Unlike most real estate associations from this era, the Edmonton Real Estate Association was able to survive through the dedication of a small group of members. The Association and its members were thus able to provide leadership to the industry when better economic times returned beginning with World War Two.

CHAPTER FOUR

War and Economic Expansion 1940-1950

Edmonton's economic recovery from the Depression began with World War Two. Unlike World War One, World War Two had a positive impact on Edmonton's economy because of the construction of the Alaska Highway, the Northwest Staging Route, Air Commonwealth training schools, and war industries such as Aircraft Repair Ltd. Another difference was that the federal and provincial governments had planned an orderly transition to peace, thus avoiding the postwar recession that had occurred in the early 1920s.

World War Two, despite its economic benefits, also imposed significant restrictions on the marketplace. The Edmonton Real Estate Association along with the real estate industry nationally became increasingly concerned about these wartime controls. The federal government's decision to prevent real estate agents charging a commission for selling land to veterans under the Veterans' Land Act was the final straw that prompted the creation of a national organization. The 1940s were also important because of the creation of the Alberta Real Estate Association (AREA).

The boom begun by the war was sustained by oil discoveries at Leduc in 1947. The oil boom began on February 13 at four o'clock when Leduc No. 1 blew in.

The drilling of other wells quickly followed. In 1951 more than three hundred wells were drilled.

Housing for the oil workers became desperate. Edmonton, Leduc, and Calmar were able to partially fill the need. Construction of the future Town of Devon began during the winter of 1947-1948 and provided more housing.

In Eric Hanson's book *Dynamic Decade*, the Leduc discovery was important because it stimulated investment in finding other reserves. It made Edmonton a refining and petrochemical centre and the main operations base for oil-industry contractors. As the scale of the industry grew in size so did the economic benefits for Edmonton.

A new generation of Edmonton real estate agents arrived in the mid-1940s and early 1950s. Many were either the sons of established Edmonton real estate agents or were people attracted to the city because of the economic opportunities generated by the development of the oil industry. Some war veterans who helped reconstruct the Edmonton real estate industry were Norm Winterburn, Stan Melton, Max Kaplan, and Don Spencer.

The Edmonton Real Estate Association began the Second World War with a

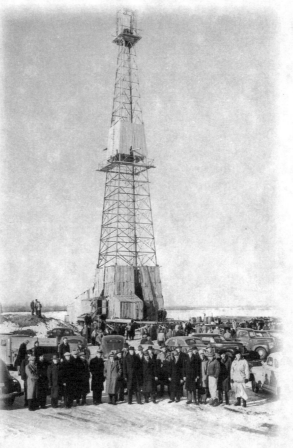

Imperial Oil Leduc number one well was completed on February 13, 1947. This event was witnessed by government and company officials, media people, and citizens of Edmonton, all anxious to be part of the most important event in the post war history of Edmonton.
(City of Edmonton Archives, EA-273-79)

The Edmonton Municipal Airport in 1944 was a busy place because of its role in the war effort. It was the location of Air Commonwealth Training Program facilities and war time industry.
(City of Edmonton Archives, BL 725/5)

Aircraft Repair Ltd. was one of the industries located at the municipal airport.
(City of Edmonton Archives, EA-10-3181.47.6)

The Association continued to operate out of the offices of its members but in 1941 it began to acquire office equipment. In November the secretary asked for a steel filing cabinet with lock and key for keeping the Association's books, files, and supplies. At the January 23, 1942, executive meeting J. Sherwin was authorized to purchase a steel three-drawer filing cabinet for $10.

membership of forty-six and a bank balance of $67.58. The membership fee was $1 and the honorarium for the secretary treasurer was $15 annually. The membership fee was increased to $2 in September 1943 and to $25 by 1951. Membership in the Association grew slowly, reaching sixty-eight members in 1951.

Administration

Standing committees continued to do much of the Association's work. The Legislative Committee worked to revise regulations for licence applications. The committee wanted the applications to be checked more carefully on who could be licensed as a real estate agent. Suggestions for revisions to the act were submitted to the provincial government for approval.

Wartime regulations

Government intervention in the market place was the new issue faced by the Edmonton Real Estate Association during the war.

Regulations included gas rationing, rental controls, housing shortages, land acquisition, and the administration of the Veterans' Land Act.

These regulations brought to a head a long-standing concern of the industry. As early as 1919 the real estate community had objected to being prevented from charging commissions on land sold to veterans. During the Depression Edmonton real estate agents had also objected to being excluded from the process of selling city-owned land.

The first indication for Edmonton real estate agents that wartime regulations would affect their business was when the Vancouver and Calgary Real Estate Boards asked for help to get a better classification for real estate agents. The way they were classified would determine the amount of gas they could get under the rationing system then in place. Both Boards argued that they needed extra to continue their business activities.

Rent controls were a more significant problem for real estate agents. They were part of a comprehensive program to control inflation. Under these regulations a landlord could not raise the rent without the consent of the Wartime Prices and Trade Board. Raising the rent was permitted when there was a substantial increase in taxes, substantial expense for improvements to the property, or wear and tear on the property.

In Edmonton the maximum rental charge was what was in effect on January 2, 1941. If the property was not rented at that time then the last rental fee in effect in 1940 would become effective. The regulations also prevented a landlord from reducing facilities or giving a tenant notice to vacate except on grounds set out in the regulations.

Initially, these regulations were not a great concern to the members of the Association since it was believed that they would not affect the rental situation in Edmonton. At a meeting of the Edmonton Real Estate Association in March 1942, George Bryan, the rental control administrator for Alberta, advised the members that these regulations were designed to "prevent the evils of inflation and unfair advantage being taken on tenants, particularly in areas where due to the presence of members of the armed forces there was a housing shortage."

In August 1942, Dominion Rentals Commissioner Cyril DeMara appealed to the Association for citizens with rooms available to charge the prevailing rental rates for the district. Since many real estate agents depended on rental income, these regulations became a source of concern.

The attitude of the Association changed drastically on December 10, 1942, when the government announced new regulations that required a tenant of a home that had been sold to be given at least twelve months' notice to vacate by the new owner. The new owner was required to prove that the property was needed for his or her own residence when the tenant left. The new regulations also clarified the position of tenants in homes that were not

Sewer construction is shown here in 1946. Although many people feared a depression after World War II, the economy actually expanded.
(City of Edmonton Archives, EA-273-82)

sold. Under the old regulations, landlords could evict tenants on three months' notice by declaring that they needed the accommodation for themselves, a relative, or an employee. After December 10, a tenant could be evicted on three months' notice only if the home was needed as the landlord's principal residence. After December 6, 1942, the rental fee of any housing not previously rented was based on the October 11, 1941, fee as the going rate.

The Association called a meeting for December 12. Stuart Darroch told the press that many real estate agents might go out of business as a result of the new regulations. He pointed to three sales that had been cancelled because of the new regulations. One of the properties was a $6,000 home in the west end. The other deals involved property in Jasper Place. A committee chaired by Andy Whyte took the Association's protest to Ottawa.

The rental controls were part of the larger problem of a housing shortage caused by no new construction during the Depression and by the influx of people to work in the war-related industries. One of the largest employers was Aircraft Repair Ltd. The plant at the municipal airport employed 500 people.

Action on the housing shortage issue by the Association began in May of 1943 following a presentation by A. J. Brown of W. H. Clark Co. and Dr. G. M. Little, City of Edmonton medical health officer. Brown discussed the extent of the housing shortage while Dr. Little explained the health implications of the situation. He said that families of four or five were living in one room in Edmonton apartments or rooming houses.

Following their presentation a resolution was passed asking the provincial government to urge the lending institutions to make loans available to Edmonton citizens to encourage new home building. If necessary the federal government might set aside the necessary funds under the National Housing Act to enable the lending institution to operate in Alberta.

The Association also supported efforts by the City of Edmonton to obtain wartime housing. Wartime Housing Ltd. was a Crown corporation with a nationwide mandate to provide housing for workers in war-related industries. Edmonton's application was finally successful and in June 1943, the sod was turned for the construction of these homes in the Ritchie district in south Edmonton. The homes erected under the project were four-, five-, and six-room dwellings.

Another concern involved land transactions for veterans. Clause 33 of the Veterans' Land Act eliminated commissions for real estate agents who sold land to veterans. This provision was designed to

Downtown Edmonton in 1947 shows the new Canadian National Railways Station, and Queen's Avenue School, which had been built before World War One.
(City of Edmonton Archives, EA-273-83)

facilitate their return to civilian life by reducing the cost of their land purchases. From the point of view of the real estate industry, this provision was another attempt to exclude real estate agents from full participation in the economy.

One success in their role as brokers at a time of government control came in the acquisition of land for Namao airport. In July 1943 the Association was asked for the names of two individuals who could provide an independent evaluation of the land to be acquired for the construction of the airport.

Canadian Real Estate Association

In the absence of any national real estate organization, real estate agents in many Canadian cities before 1943 participated in the activities of the National Real Estate Association, an American-based organization established in 1892.

The 1913 convention of this organization was held in Winnipeg where a code of ethics was adopted.

Members of the Edmonton Real Estate Association attended a meeting on the founding of the Canadian Association of Real Estate Boards, now known as the Canadian Real Estate Association (CREA) in January 1943. Delegates from various parts of Canada attended the meeting held in Ottawa. Andy Whyte and Stuart Darroch represented the Edmonton Real Estate Association as well as the real estate boards in Medicine Hat, Regina, Moose Jaw, and Calgary.

Andy Whyte was particularly enthusiastic about this first step on the national level towards organized real estate. In an article in *The Canadian Realtor* published twenty-five years later, Whyte recalled that: *"to own one's own home [was] a growing desire and real active real estate boards should be on the alert to sense the trend [in building styles] and layout of districts and many other features which we have not, up to the moment, thought of."*

A joint meeting followed between these delegates and the Ontario group, and CREA was officially created shortly thereafter. At the founding meeting, Andy Whyte was elected to be the first regional vice-president for the West, which in 1943 included all the territory west of Thunder Bay.

With Edmonton's membership in CREA it could now make official use of various terms and logos. The terms REALTOR and MLS® and their logos are subject to strict guidelines on their use. The term REALTOR refers to real estate professionals in Canada who are members of the Canadian Real Estate Association and The National Association of

Realtors in the United States. They subscribe to a high standard of professional service and to a strict Code of Ethics. The term is not a synonym for broker/agent or salesperson or for any other real estate professional calling. Members in Canada are licensed by the Canadian Real Estate Association to use the REALTOR marks in connection with themselves and their industry.

Local boards were discouraged from admitting people who were not engaged in the real estate business. The real estate business includes real estate brokerage, property management, mortgage financing, real estate appraising, land development, and building.

REALTOR and MLS® are registered trademarks licensed for use by REALTORS. Strict guidelines on their design and presentation highlight their status, significance, and special meaning to the public.

Edmonton hosted its first CREA convention in 1955. One of the significant developments at the 1955 conference was the founding of the Canadian Institute of Realtors (CIR). The charter members of the organization from Edmonton were Stan Melton, Bob Grierson, Don Spencer, Jack Weber and Norm Winterburn.

Alberta Real Estate Association

Prior to AREA a provincial real estate association existed in Alberta. It was established during the pre-World War One boom. Little information is available on its organization, membership, or activities. All that is known is that it survived through to the mid-1920s and was based in Calgary.

In the early 1920s some Alberta real estate agents and salesmen were part of the Inter-State Realty Association, which included the states of Washington, Oregon, Idaho, and Montana, and the provinces of Alberta and British Columbia. Its main objective was the passage of legislation providing for the licensing and bonding of real estate salesmen.

Interest in re-establishing a provincial association was evident during the 1930s. In March 1931, Frank Lorimer on behalf of the Edmonton Real Estate Association met with the Calgary Real Estate Board where he conveyed his hope of forming a provincial association. In October 1939, Sam Ferris in his presidential address suggested making arrangements for a provincial meeting. In February 1940, a committee was appointed to plan a convention for the spring. The meeting never took place.

The establishment of AREA began at a meeting held at the Buffalo Hotel in Red Deer on June 19, 1946. Andy Whyte organized it. The Edmonton delegation consisted of Andy Whyte, J. C. Kenwood, president of the Edmonton Real Estate Association, J. Sherwin, Mark Cummings, Stuart Darroch, Sam Ferris, Sid Lawrie, and Luke Winterburn.

At the meeting, Andy Whyte reviewed the first attempt before World War One to establish

REALTOR®

MULTIPLE LISTING SERVICE®

LADIES SECTION
12TH ANNUAL
CANADIAN ASS'N. OF REAL ESTATE BOARDS
HILLCREST COUNTRY CLUB

Meeting of the ladies section of the Canadian Real Estate Association at the Hillcrest Country Club, September 21, 1955.
(Edmonton Real Estate Board)

a provincial real estate association. Whyte then called for opinions from the delegates on the need for a provincial real estate board. The Edmonton delegation was unanimous in its support. Sam Ferris thought that real estate agents and sales staff should be organized as chartered accountants, doctors, dentists, and lawyers are and that the provincial organization be linked with CREA. Kenwood thought that the industry through this organization could help the provincial government draft legislation for the mutual benefit of real estate agents and the general public.

Given the unanimous support for an organization, the meeting moved on to the work of creating AREA. This work involved dividing the province for organizational purposes, setting membership fees, and writing a constitution. It was agreed that Edmonton would organize the territory north of Didsbury. The issues of fees was to be resolved by the board of directors, who were to be elected at the next meeting.

Mark Cummings introduced a draft of a constitution that included a code of ethics based on the Ontario Provincial Real Estate Board and the Ontario Licensing Act. He continued his work as chairman of the Constitution, Bylaws and Code of Ethics Committee.

With the success of this planning meeting, they decided to call a general meeting for all licensed real estate agents and salesmen of the Province of Alberta for September 7, 1946, in Red Deer.

The reasons for creating an organization as outlined by Whyte remained consistent with those defined as early as 1909 and 1926. These reasons were:

1. To assist in desirable legislation affecting real estate;
2. To raise and unify the standard of the real estate profession;
3. To cultivate acquaintanceship and good will among the real estate brokers of the province;
4. To sponsor fair dealings in real estate transactions;
5. To acquaint the public with the prevailing high ethics of the real estate profession;
6. To increase confidence and security for the investor of Alberta real estate both urban and rural in their transactions with bona fide brokers.

The meeting also elected officers for the new Association. The executive consisted of a president, two vice-presidents, a secretary-treasurer, and five directors. The nominating committee recommended Andy Whyte for president but he declined in favour of Kenneth Lyle. In recognition of Whyte's contribution to organized real estate he was nominated for the position of honorary president, which he accepted. (Whyte would remain active in the Association until he was ninety-four, serving on a variety of committees.) Other Edmontonians elected to the first executive were Lou Weber, who served as vice-president, Mark Cummings, Stuart Darroch, and Sam Ferris, all of whom served as directors.

In addition to Edmonton real estate agents serving on the executive, Tom McGee also served on the interim Constitution, Bylaws and Code of Ethics Committee chaired by Mark Cummmings.

One of the final acts of the meeting was to set the dues at $2 per year, which were collected immediately by Sam Ferris and turned over to the new secretary-treasurer, Howard Kelly.

The newly elected executive of AREA first met at the Hotel Macdonald on November 1, 1946. A uniform commission schedule for the province was discussed. The Edmonton Real Estate Association and the Calgary Real Estate Board were to be approached on conforming with AREA's schedule. Lou Weber also suggested a membership drive and he volunteered to write a letter to all licensed salesman and agents in the Edmonton area encouraging them to join.

Edmonton real estate agents also contributed to the second general meeting of AREA. Mark Cummings spoke on the constitution and bylaws prepared by his committee. Stuart Darroch, successor to Andy Whyte as the regional vice-president of CREA, discussed the history of real estate boards and encouraged Albertans to participate in the national association. CREA complimented him on his role as their representative by sending him a telegram: *"congratulating the real estate men of the West for their speedy advances."*

Lou Weber then presented an interim commission schedule, which was approved after revisions were suggested from the floor. Andy Whyte reported on the success that the Association had achieved via the Legislative Committee on revising the new Real Estate Agents' Licensing Act. Whyte reported to the meeting: *"that the fullest Government Co-*

operation was being given to the REALTORS, [which was in turn] soliciting the REALTORS co-operation . . . to bring in this new act."

Other Edmonton representatives at this meeting introduced issues that reflected local interest in national concerns. Luke Winterburn suggested that AREA should write to Mr. Donald Gordon for immediate relief on rent controls. The president noted that there was a letter on file from CREA stating that they had a committee working with Ottawa and asking them not to make any individual appeal at this time.

At subsequent meetings of the Association during the 1940s, new listing forms were prepared based on the forms then in use in Calgary and Edmonton. The Association continued to strengthen its links to CREA by appointing Andy Whyte to the board of CREA to represent AREA.

The participation of Edmonton real estate agents in AREA did carry with it certain hazards. At one meeting Stuart Darroch presented a motion resolving that: *"Premier Manning and the Minister of Public Works be informed of the most appalling condition of the highway between Edmonton and Red Deer and that the Minister of Public Works be instructed to take immediate action to correct this situation and that tourists be warned of the condition of the road in the meantime."* The motion was lost.

The first annual convention of the Alberta Real Estate Association was held in Calgary in 1947.
(Edmonton Real Estate Board)

1st Annual Convention Alberta Real Estate Association Palliser Hotel. Calgary. Oct 3rd 1947.

Edmonton hosted its first AREA conference on September 24, 1948. At this meeting Sam Ferris was elected president and Andy Whyte honorary president. Sid Lawrie was elected secretary-treasurer and Norm Winterburn was director.

The AREA conference had presentations on the national Housing Act; Fred Scott spoke on legal points. The convention included a reception followed by a banquet at the Hotel Macdonald.

The total cost of the convention was $616.33. This sum included $497.55 for the banquet. Sundry expenses for printing of tickets and programmes were $78.78, and Fred Scott's expenses and his fee to attend the conference totalled $60.

By 1946 Edmonton had 147 licensed real estate agents as members of AREA — the largest number from any community. In 1955 Edmonton still had the largest contingent in AREA, with 162 members out of a total membership of 439. In 1956 Edmontonians made up 211 of the membership total of 515.

The Edmonton Real Estate Association during the 1940s shifted from simply surviving to aggressively pursuing a number of objectives. It participated in the formation of CREA and AREA. It also helped the effort to oppose the clause in the Veterans' Land Act which prevented the charging of commissions. It also took an interest in the wartime housing problems of Edmontonians. Housing had become a problem during the Second World War because of the lack of new construction during the Depression, restrictions on new house construction, and the influx of workers and military personnel involved in the war effort.

Despite the economic recovery of the 1940s which was continued after the War by the discovery of oil at Leduc in 1947, the membership remained small. Organized real estate, however, was poised for a spectacular period of growth as the extent of the Leduc discovery became known in the 1950s.

Stony Plain Road and 149 Street in 1948: 149 Street was the boundary between Edmonton and Jasper Place prior to annexation in 1964.
(City of Edmonton Archives, EA-10-166)

In 1948, the Alberta Real Estate Association Conference was held on September 24 at Hotel MacDonald.
(Edmonton Real Estate Board)

CHAPTER FIVE

A Golden Age for Edmonton Real Estate 1951-1981

In 1951 Edmonton entered a golden age of spectacular growth, unprecedented in its history. A population explosion, a new civic centre, new subdivisions, and new suburbs transformed this city and the metropolitan area. Edmonton became a major centre for the petrochemical industry and expanded its traditional role as a government, educational, and transportation centre. Expectations since the early 1880s that a great city would be built on the banks of the North Saskatchewan River were realized.

Edmonton's expansion was reflected in the rapid growth of the real estate industry and substantial changes in its organization. The Edmonton Real Estate Association was replaced by an entirely new organization. The Edmonton Real Estate Board Co-operative listing Bureau, established in 1952, dramatically increased the services offered to its members. It established permanent offices to carry out its expanded role within the city of Edmonton and the province.

Edmonton in the golden age

The economic expansion of the golden age was partly due to ongoing oil exploration and development. This discovery phase reached its peak in 1952 when 551 wells were drilled. The last major discovery of a conventional source of oil during this era was the Pembina field, located 85 miles (137 kilometres) southwest of Edmonton. The first large-scale efforts to develop the oil sands in the Fort McMurray area began in 1964 with the construction of the Great Canadian Oil Sands plant. It went into production in 1967.

Added to the direct economic benefits of the oil boom were increased construction and expanded educational facilities. Student enrolment increased at the University of Alberta and its infrastructure grew. New additions to the campus included the Henry Marshall Tory Building (1966), which was named after the first president of this institution.

The Northern Alberta Institution of Technology (NAIT) opened in 1963. NAIT's courses were designed to train students in practical ways that were directly applicable to the job market.

New provincial government services and jobs also contributed to Edmonton's booming

The postwar boom transformed downtown Edmonton. The new buildings in this 1967 photograph include the CN Tower, City Hall, and the Centennial Library.
(Provincial Archives of Alberta, J 97/2)

Originally constructed in 1911 for Alexander Cameron Rutherford, Rutherford House is now a designated historic site on the campus of the University of Alberta.
(Edmonton Real Estate Board)

Jasper Avenue looking east from 101 Street in 1966 shows the new Empire Block under construction.
(City of Edmonton Archives, EA-273-8)

economy. Existing departments such as Highways expanded to meet the increased transportation needs of the province. A new department, Culture, Youth & Recreation, was created to deal with the development of Alberta's cultural and historical resources.

The demand for housing went up as Edmonton's population grew from 159,631 in 1951 to 551,314 in 1982. Unlike the undeveloped subdivisions of pre-World War One, the new subdivisions were rapidly filled with new arrivals. The effect on Edmonton's boundaries was dramatic. Since 1917, city boundaries had remained unchanged simply because the pre-World War One boom had created an oversupply of undeveloped land. Fringe communities, such as Beverly and Jasper Place, remained without many of the city services. By the 1950s, however, the mood of Edmonton (along with that of the entire nation) shifted to expansion, since most of the land from the boom had been used up. Extending Edmonton's boundaries resumed in 1947 with the annexation of Pleasantview and continued until 1982, which increased Edmonton's size from 40.8 to 270.5 square miles (65.7 to 435.3 square kilometres).

Real estate was an excellent investment during the 1960s and particularly in the 1970s. The widespread land speculation evident before World War One was replaced by land investment that was actually developed for residential, commercial or industrial use. According to the City of Edmonton Planning Department, the real value of property increased 36 percent during the years 1962 to 1969 and 92 percent in the 1970s. This increase resulted in the price of the average home in Edmonton going from $12,556 in 1962 to $91,438 in 1981.

New buildings

One effect of this growth was a program to rebuild the city, particularly in the downtown core. Many buildings constructed during the railway boom of 1900 to 1914 were demolished and replaced with modern ones. One objective was to design and build a civic centre with a central park surrounded by public buildings.

A civic centre had been planned since 1912, but the high cost of land and the Depression had delayed its construction. In 1927 the old Edmonton Real Estate Association had tried to persuade the land owners to cooperate with the city by providing the land at a lower price, but they had refused. The civic centre begun in 1956 thus fulfils an old objective.

The civic centre includes Churchill Square, a new city hall, library, art gallery, and theatre. These buildings transformed the appearance of the City of Edmonton's downtown core. The Edmonton City Hall (completed in 1956) was the first step in this development. It was a controversial addition. Critics disliked its modernism while defenders saw it as a symbol of Edmonton's progress.

The Citadel Theatre had begun in the old Salvation Army Citadel building on 102nd Street in 1965. In 1976 it moved to a new facility on Churchill Square. Its initial construction and subsequent expansion was funded by both private and public contributions.

New commercial structures in the downtown core began in 1949, when the Hotel Macdonald was expanded. The *Edmonton Journal,* in commenting on the addition, noted that the old portion: *"will be overshadowed by this far-from-beautiful sixteen-storey rectangular mass."* It opened in 1953. Other commercial buildings downtown were the new Empire Block (opened in 1963), the twenty-six storey CN Tower (completed in 1966) and Edmonton Centre (completed in 1974). The last major addition during the golden age was Manulife Place (completed in 1983).

The Hotel Macdonald and the MacLeod Building built before World War One linked the city with its past. The Hotel Macdonald had been completed by the Grand Trunk Pacific Railway in 1916. The MacLeod Building, completed in 1915 by Edmonton businessman Kenneth MacLeod, had been Edmonton's tallest building until the construction of the Hotel Macdonald addition in 1951.

Portions of the former City of Strathcona were also preserved during this period. Some of the buildings on both sides of Whyte Avenue

Top:
An addition to the Hotel Macdonald was under construction in 1951. This was the first major addition to downtown Edmonton since the construction of the Canadian National Railways station in 1928.
(City of Edmonton Archives, EA-273-33)

Middle:
Westmount Shopping Centre in 1969 was the first mall to be built in suburban Edmonton during the postwar boom.
(City of Edmonton Archives, EA-267-47)

Bottom:
The Edmonton Coliseum built in the mid 1970s was one of many new sports facilities built during the golden age.
(City of Edmonton Archives, EA-117-145)

between 103rd and 104th streets are still part of the commercial core. Public buildings such as the library and the fire hall have also survived and still operate.

New sports facilities were built for the Commonwealth Games in 1978 when

Edmonton was the host city. One was the Commonwealth Stadium, containing more than 42,000 seats. The Edmonton Coliseum, where the Edmonton Oilers hockey team plays, was also opened in 1975. Improvements were made to the Exhibition grounds as well.

Calder, Highlands, and Allendale. In some cases where development had not begun, the original subdivision plan was cancelled and the district redesigned to reflect current ideas on town planning. Districts that went through this process included North Glenora and Argyll. These subdivisions were the first to witness the boom in residential construction.

Jasper Place occupied land that had been originally subdivided in 1910 but development did not take place for another forty years. In 1948 building permits valued at $327,225 were issued, which included eighty-one new homes. Life in Jasper Place during the boom meant some people had no running water, no bus service, no sewers, and no indoor plumbing. Given the rate of growth, Jasper Place quickly evolved from a village to a town. It amalgamated with Edmonton in 1961.

Beverly, on the northeast boundary of Edmonton, was originally incorporated as a village in 1913 with a population of 300. Its population reached 1,000 by 1929 where it remained until the boom in the 1940s and 1950s. At the time of amalgamation with Edmonton in 1961 it had a population of 9,041. It lacked urban services just as Jasper Place had. Water and sewerage services were delayed until 1953.

Old districts

Some of the neighbourhoods developed during the golden age had origins dating back to the pre-World War One boom. These included Westmount, Jasper Place, Beverly,

New districts

The development of entirely new districts within the city limits was also a feature of Edmonton's growth during this period. The first of the new districts was Pleasantview. The portion of Pleasantview east of 106 Street had been part of Edmonton since 1914. The remaining portion was annexed in 1947. It was subdivided into one-half to full acre lots and sold under the Veterans' Land Act to war veterans. Later these new districts proved to be particularly popular with the baby boomers.

Other new districts developed in rapid succession through to the early 1980s. From

Valleyview in the west to Capilano in the east and from Castle Downs in the north to Mill Woods in the south, Edmonton was expanding in all directions. Two of the most ambitious developments were Castle Downs and Mill Woods. Both projects began in the early 1970s for a planned residential population of 200,000. Both subdivisions differed radically from all previous ones. They represented the trend towards total concept planning. This means that several housing types, commercial buildings, institutions, and parks were planned at one time. Another feature of both projects was the reservation of land for a town centre that incorporated commercial, institutional, and high-density residential land uses. One difference between the two projects was that Castle Downs was designed and developed entirely by a private company while Mill Woods was designed by the City of Edmonton and then private companies were able to develop the individual lots.

In 1970, Mill Woods was the largest publicly sponsored land assembly project in North America. In that year, the provincial government purchased 4,425 acres (1,790 hectares) and then sold the land to the City of Edmonton in 1971 for residential development. The intent of the land assembly was to develop and maintain a large supply of housing lots to limit rapid increases in housing prices.

The first distribution of land in the Mill Woods subdivision was made on a first-come-first-served basis in April 1973. This event, in terms of its public interest, had some resemblance to the famous 1912 Hudson's Bay

Co. land sale. The line up began to form at 2 p.m. although the sale did not begin until 9:30 a.m. the following day. As the *Edmonton Journal* noted: *"lawn chairs, sleeping cots, card tables, coffee thermoses and even one television set were strung out in rough fashion on the city hall's main floor as the prospective home owners played cards and reviewed subdivision plans during the night."*

Malls developed along with suburbs. They served the existing population and encouraged further residential and commercial development in the area. This trend began in Edmonton between 1953 and 1955 when Westmount Shoppers Park was built. David Gray, a vice-president with Shoppers Park Westmount Ltd., said that: *"retailers found that increased sales resulted from merchandise being made more accessible to the shopper."* He also noted that shopping centres enhanced downtown business by reducing traffic congestion. Westmount proved to be a success — it expanded in 1979. Similar commercial developments began in other parts of the city. These included Bonnie Doon Mall in 1958, Northgate in 1963, Southgate in 1967,

The Princess Theatre in Old Strathcona was constructed in 1914 by John McKernan. It was an exceptional example of commercial architecture since its facade featured British Columbia marble. It has been restored as part of the renewal of Old Strathcona.
(Edmonton Real Estate Board)

The former Fire Hall Number One of the City of Strathcona was renovated in 1974 for use by the Walterdale Theatre.
(Edmonton Real Estate Board)

Gainer Block in Old Strathcona was constructed by pioneer industrialist John Gainer in 1902. It was restored as part of the overall renewal of Whyte Avenue between 104th and 103rd Streets.
(Edmonton Real Estate Board)

Londonderry in 1972, and Heritage Mall in 1981.

West Edmonton Mall, built in the 1980s, was the last of these types of commercial

West Edmonton Mall as it appeared with the completion of phase three in 1986.
(West Edmonton Mall Administration)

Walk-up apartments of the type featured in this picture were constructed in large numbers in the golden age.
(City of Edmonton Archives, EA-33-295)

developments. Triple Five Corporation, owned by the Ghermezian family, built the complex over a six-year period in three phases, beginning in 1980. It was the largest mall in the world. Phase One, which opened in 1981, is 1,150,000 square feet (107,000 square metres), which provided space for 220 stores and services. Its interior furnishings include inlaid Italian marble floors and an enormous chandelier. West Edmonton Mall, however, is not only distinctive for its size and its decor. It also introduced a new form of retailing by providing a range of services (including recreational facilities) unparalleled in any other mall in North America. It has become a major Edmonton tourist destination in its own right. Real estate spin offs include housing

developments such as West Edmonton Village — a multi-family development.

Bedroom communities

As access to Edmonton improved, places like Stony Plain, Spruce Grove, St. Albert, Fort Saskatchewan, Leduc, and Sherwood Park were able to expand.

Stony Plain began in 1905 as a town on the Canadian Northern Railway line. Spruce Grove was established as a townsite on the Grand Trunk Pacific line in 1912. Both communities served the local farming community before evolving into Edmonton bedroom communities in the early 1970s. Stony Plain became a town in 1971 and Spruce Grove became a city in 1986.

St. Albert was established in 1861 as a mission settlement by Father Albert Lacombe. Lacombe's original log church, built in 1861, and the bishop's residence, built in 1888, still stand as historic and religious sites. It is one of Alberta's oldest communities and Edmonton's largest suburb. It became a city in 1977.

Fort Saskatchewan owes its origins to the establishment of an RCMP detachment in 1875 and to the fact that the Canadian Northern Railway passed through the community on its way to Edmonton. In 1899 Fort Saskatchewan was incorporated as a village and in 1904 it became a town. It remained a quiet country place until 1954 when Sherritt Gordon Mines Ltd. established their multi-million-dollar nickel refinery. Since 1954 other industries have been established, making it a significant industrial centre. It became a city in 1985.

The history of Leduc begins in 1867 when a telegraph station was built and named in memory of a well-known pioneer priest, Father Leduc. A townsite was established by the Calgary and Edmonton Railway in the 1890s. The discovery of the Leduc oil field in 1947 has been the basis of its growth since the Second World War. It became a city in 1983.

Sherwood Park, once known as Campbelltown, was originally proposed by developer and entrepreneur John Hook Campbell in the early 1950s. The first preview of homes was opened to the public on

September 10, 1955. The home show featured sixty-eight ranch-style homes designed by J. Thomas Wilner of Los Angeles and C.T. Larrington of Edmonton. The homes were advertised in the *Edmonton Journal* for $10,459 to $14,100. Payments were from $59.62 per month. These homes featured built-in eye-level wall ovens, countertop stoves, and double compartment sinks with swing spout. The exclusive agent for Campbelltown Realty Ltd. was Spencer and Grierson Ltd. This was a well-established firm in the Edmonton area.

From this beginning, Sherwood Park has become a significant community in the Edmonton metropolitan area, reaching a population of 29,000 by the early 1980s. The last neighbourhood to be developed during the golden age was Village on the Lake, which features an artificial lake. Along with residential development, Sherwood Park has also acquired two shopping centres and a range of educational and recreational facilities.

Real estate specialiation

The boom made specialization in the real estate industry possible. Real estate agents before the 1950s had to combine real estate with insurance to survive. Not only could a company work solely in real estate, it could also specialize in various types of real estate, such as condominiums and high-end/low-end single family homes. Acreages, recreational property, and commercial real estate were also specialities.

Esch Real Estate specialized in acreages. Started by Peter Esch, it was continued by his sons Ron and Jim. (Jim remains active in the EREB and has been given a Life Membership.) Most of the acreages were located west and east of Winterburn and Stony Plain. Peter Esch recalls that many of his customers were from a rural background who wanted to return to the land.

Initially, people were interested in three-acre hobby farms where they could raise animals and have their privacy. This trend was encouraged by the County of Parkland, which benefited from the expansion of its tax base. It limited acreages initially to three-acre parcels. Esch Real Estate helped farmers market and sell their land, thus creating economic benefits for the land owners as well as for the county.

The Laurier Heights district in 1970 shows typical residential development during the golden age.
(City of Edmonton Archives, EA-33-143)

MacGregor Real Estate was a company that specialized in recreational properties. It was established by Bill MacGregor in 1944. He was a member of the original group that set up the Edmonton Real Estate Board Co-operative Listing Bureau, Ltd. in 1952. He was awarded a Life Membership in the EREB.

Bill began to sell lake front property in the late 1940s, eventually establishing an office at Alberta Beach in 1952. As with acreages, the customers had to be educated on the finer points of this type of real estate. In some cases the property line extended to the beach and in other cases it did not. The distinction between a lake front lot and a genuine lake front lot depended on the survey plan.

Expertise gathered by the Esch family, Bill MacGregor, and others was passed on to various companies through the activities of the Board's Acreages, Farms and Recreational Properties Committee. This educational program for members of the industry was necessary because acreages are a specialized market that

The actual development, not just the promotion of new subdivisions on the outskirts of Edmonton was an important aspect of Edmonton real estate in the golden age.
(City of Edmonton Archives, EA-33-167)

have specific needs concerning water problems, septic systems, schools, zoning regulations, and utilities.

Industrial, commercial, and investment property was another specialization. Three companies active in this area were Melton Real Estate, Weber Brothers, and Imperial Real Estate. Pat Turner was in charge of Melton's commercial division. He contributed to the

49

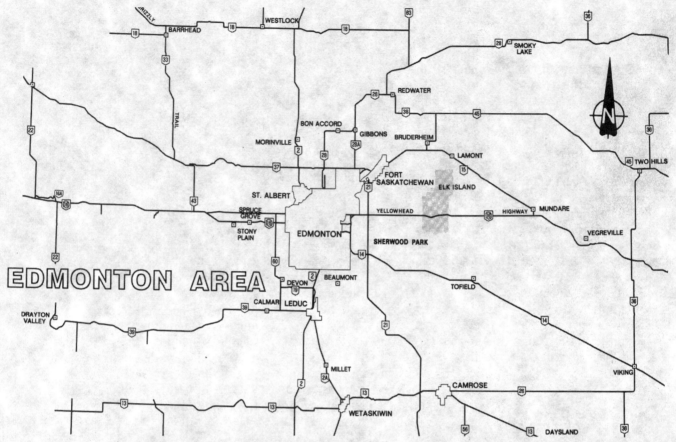

activities of the Edmonton Real Estate Board by serving on the Industrial, Commercial and Investment standing committee.

Imperial Real Estate was established by Jack Young in 1952. Dennis Stewart, Ray Buxton, and John Sinclair were managers of its various branches. In 1958 Dennis Stewart acquired the company and expanded it to twelve departments. These departments dealt with all aspects of the industry.

Many of the employees of Imperial Real Estate played an important part in the activities of the Association. This group included Ray Buxton, Dennis Stewart, and Trevor Caithness. Trevor Caithness was with the company from 1958 to 1967, when he went into business for himself. One of the distinctive features of the company, he recalls, was Ray Buxton's eighty-hour training program.

Edmonton Real Estate Board Co-operative Listing Bureau

The organization of Edmonton's real estate industry began to change when Edmonton delegates came back from a CREA conference in Quebec City in 1951. These delegates returned with ideas about education and a multiple listing service that would transform the real estate industry in Edmonton over the next thirty years.

Norm Winterburn played a leading role in this process of change. During the convention, he attended a presentation by Phil Seagrove (of the Hamilton Real Estate Board) on the subject of a multiple listing service. He liked the idea because it gave the opportunity for the Edmonton Real Estate Association to provide a new service to its members. He returned determined to see the creation of a similar institution in Edmonton.

The idea of a multiple listing bureau in Edmonton was presented to the general membership at a meeting on March 31, 1952, where it was greeted unenthusiastically. George Sillman moved that no attempt should be made to actually complete a co-operative listing bureau unless they had first obtained a favourable majority vote of the members at a general meeting called for that purpose.

Despite some opposition within the Edmonton Real Estate Board, a meeting of interested members led to the creation of a co-operative listing bureau. At a meeting on May

1, the chairman presented the rules and regulations, and discussion about a seven percent sales commission followed. Weber said that it was financially impossible to start the bureau on anything less than seven percent.

The Edmonton Real Estate Board Co-operative Listing Bureau Ltd. was officially incorporated on June 27, 1952, under "The Co-operative Associations Act, 1946." (See appendices for Certificate of Incorporation.) The founding members were Norm Winterburn, Mark Cummings, Jack Haliburton, Sid Lawrie, Jack Weber, Stan Melton, Don Spencer, Frank Alloway, Bill MacGregor, and Tom Visser.

The Edmonton Real Estate Board Co-operative Listing Bureau Ltd. operated as a separate organization with its own executive. It worked closely with the old Edmonton Real Estate Association. It had the same membership and had the same need for permanent offices and a permanent staff.

Amalgamation of the Association and the Co-op

The integration of the two organizations began by sharing information. On August 27, 1952, Jack Haliburton, chairman of the Co-op, reported to the Edmonton Real Estate Board that the Bureau had been in operation for exactly three weeks and during that time 89 listings had been taken, of which 5 had been sold and another 4 sales were in the process of being completed, making a total of 9 sales out of 89 for ten percent. He said that they had received some criticism and complaints and also a few pats on the back. Haliburton felt that the Edmonton Real Estate Board Co-operative Listing Bureau would be beneficial to all.

Cooperation moved from sharing information to integrating the two organizations. In September 1953 the Edmonton Real Estate Board began by adopting two forms used by the Co-op: the offer-to-purchase form and the listing form.

Membership of the two organizations was the same from the executive to the general membership. By December 1953, new applicants to the Co-op were advised that approval of their applications for membership in the Board would mean automatic approval of their Co-op application. By May 1955, Secretary Henry Flewwelling advised that there

were eighty member agents in the Edmonton Real Estate Board, fifty-four of whom were also members of the Co-op Bureau.

In July 1954, the Edmonton Real Estate Board wrote to the Co-op asking them for office space and a permanent secretary. In September the Co-op offered to supply permanent secretarial services to the Edmonton Real Estate Board for $50 per month and that in addition the Board was to pay all out-of-pocket expenses for stationery, postage, and audits. The new arrangement would come into effect on January 1, 1955. The offer was accepted and on January 28, 1955, the Edmonton Real Estate Board held its first meeting in the Wallace building, with Henry Flewwelling serving as secretary.

On May 10, 1955, the two organizations had their first joint meeting. They shared information on membership and discussed common problems. The most important one was the lack of attendance at the general meetings of both organizations. Suggestions included giving tickets to the principals of large firms and making them responsible for the attendance of their sales personnel. It was also suggested that the tickets be sold two weeks in advance. Stan Melton went so far as to suggest that the Edmonton Real Estate Board bill each firm for an amount equal to fifty percent of their sales staff for tickets to each general meeting. The suggestion was withdrawn for lack of a seconder.

Norm Winterburn said that Phil Seagrove of Hamilton, Ontario, would arrive in Edmonton on May 30 for a joint meeting of the two organizations. (Phil Seagrove's presentation was part of the Co-operative Bureau's ongoing efforts to popularize the use of the multiple-listing service. In his presentation he stressed the need to have one organization to represent the industry.)

The final point discussed at this joint meeting was the fact that some salesmen were placing advertisements in the *Edmonton Journal* without naming the employee's firm. All agents were to be notified that this was contrary to section 25A of the Real Estate Agents' Licensing Act. Any further complaints were to be turned over to the superintendent of insurance.

A committee chaired by Henry Flewwelling brought about the formal amalgamation of the two organizations. The first annual meeting of the Edmonton Real Estate Board Co-operative

The first listing of the Multiple Listing Service was taken by Norm Winterburn on August 7, 1952.
(Edmonton Real Estate Board)

The first MLS® listing at 11158 - 65 Street sold in five days for $13,700.
(Edmonton Real Estate Board)

BUREAU COPY

EXCLUSIVE AUTHORITY TO SELL
CO-OPERATIVE LISTING AGREEMENT

To *L. Winterburn & Son*
and to Members Edmonton Real Estate Board Co-operative Listing Bureau Limited.

In consideration of you listing and offering for sale the undermentioned property and agreeing to list it for sale with all Broke Members of the Edmonton Real Estate Board Co-operative Listing Bureau Limited, I hereby give you the sole and exclusive listing thereof, with sole authority to dispose of the same irrevocably until the _____ day of *Sept* A.D. 19 *52*, at the price and on the terms herein stated or as may be agreed upon.

LOCATION   No. *11158*   Street *65th*   Lot *19*   Block *22*   Plan *600-U*
Subject to the reservations, covenants, conditions and exceptions contained in the existing Certificate of Title.

Owner(s) full name(s) *Jas. G. Taylor*

POSSESSION   Possession to be given _____ days from the date of sale of *main floor* _____ day of _____ 195 _____
subject to the rights of tenants, if any.

Taxes, Rents, Interest and Insurance to be adjusted at the date of sale if rented, otherwise at the date of possession.

PRICE   Price (including commission) *Thirteen Thousand Seven Hundred* Dollars ($ *13,700*).
Cash payment *Eight Thousand* Dollars ($ *8,000*)
Balance $ *80.00* monthly including interest at *6* percent.
Or, balance payable as follows:

The following appurtenances shall be included in the sale price *Gas radiant in living room main floor & all chattels in basement suite which do not belong to the tenant.*

COMMISSION   I agree to pay you a commission of Seven (7%) percent of the sale price on any sale/exchange effected during the currency of this exclusive listing either by myself or by any other person, or in the event of a sale or exchange resulting from negotiations commenced or instituted during the currency of this listing, or, in the event that I should fail for any reason to complete the sale upon you introducing a potential purchaser, able, ready and willing to deal on the prescribed terms or such other terms as may be agreed upon by myself from time to time. In consideration of your endeavours to sell I hereby charge this property with any commission which may be earned under the terms herein. In the event of a sale, any necessary documents shall be prepared at my expense.

It is agreed that should the Purchaser make a deposit but fail to complete the purchase your full commission shall nevertheless be deemed to be earned but my liability shall not in that event exceed the amount of the deposit, or if I fail to accept purchaser's offer on these terms your commission shall be deemed to be earned.

It is understood and agreed that all enquiries from any source whatsoever will be referred to you.

I agree to allow you to show prospective purchasers over the property during reasonable hours, and I hereby give you the exclusive right to place a "FOR SALE" sign upon the property.

I have read and clearly understand the above listing agreement and I acknowledge having received a copy of it on this date

OTHER AGENTS   It is understood and agreed that in the event of a sale being made by any member of the Co-operative Listing Bureau all the terms of this Agreement shall apply, and the commission as provided for will be payable by me to *L. Winterburn & Son* and to no one else and further that you, _____ *Winterburn & Son* will be solely responsible for reimbursing such other member of the Bureau in accordance with the arrangements in effect between you and the Bureau.

STRIKE OUT ONE LINE   Appointments to be made only by *H. Kaye & L. Winterburn & Son*
Or appointments may be made by any Bureau Member.

DATED this *6th* day of *Aug* 19 *52*   OWNER *Jas G. Taylor*

_____ *M. Winterburn*
(Witness)   OWNER (or Spouse) _____

Copy hereof received _____   Address *11344 - 72th*

Phone: Res. *75936*   Office *Nil*

(FOR DESCRIPTION OF PROPERTY SEE REVERSE SIDE)

CO-OP. No. *E.1*   Appointments through _____   ROOMS (No.) *5 on main floor*
EXPIRES   BEDRS. *2 on main floor - 2 in basement suite*
September 20th, 1952   *L. Winterburn & Son*   SUITES *4 room suite with private bath in basement*

No. *11158*   STREET *65th Street*   DISTRICT *Bellevue*   Price *$13,700.00*
Cash pmt. *$8000.00* Bal. *$80.00* per mo

Lot *19*   Blk. *22*   Storeys *1*   Style *Bungalow*   Mtge. _____ Int. % *6*

Plan *600-U* Age *7 yr*   Insul. (Walls) *Yes* (Ceil.) *Yes*   Payable to *Vendor*
Size Lot *33. 123*   Exterior Finish *stucco* Roof *patent*   Pmt. per Mo. _____ Taxes: *$213.76*
Size House *x*   Color *Pebble dash* Exposure *East*
Thermo. _____ Gravity or _____ yes

MAIN FLR.—Vest. *yes*   Hall *yes* L. Room *Yes*   BASEMENT *Full basement with 4 room suite*
Fireplace, etc. *Tile-gas radiant*   Oak in L.R. & D.R.   *with private bath rented at $70.00*
Dining Rm. *x*   Maple in Bedrooms   *per month.*
no
Sun Rm. *no*   Bed Rs. (1) *yes*   INCL. IN PRICE (Chattels, etc.) *Gas radiant in*
(2) *yes*   (3) *x*   *living room on main floor and all*
Bath R. *Rainbow tile on walls & rubber tile on floors*   *chattels in basement suite which do*
2nd. FLR.   Bed. Rs. (1) _____ (2) _____   *not belong to the tenant.*
(3) *x*   Bath R. _____   GARAGE *yes*   Fir. _____ Htd. *yes* Walks *yes*
General Condition, Appearance and Remarks: GROUNDS—Landscaped? *yes* Fenced? *yes*
Newly decorated throughout, floors   Distance to Sch. _____ Stores *½ blk* Bus *½ blk*
newly sanded   Poss'n? *Main floor immediately*   Key? *L. Winterburn & Son*

Owner *Jas. G. Taylor*   Address *11344 - 72nd St.*   Ph. Res. *75936* Bus. _____
Date *August 6th, 1952*   Listing Broker *L. Winterburn & Son*

BUREAU COPY

The Edmonton Real Estate Board
Co-operative Listing Bureau,
304 Wallace Bldg.,
Edmonton, Alberta.

Co-op No. *E-1*   Price *13,700.00*
Address *11158 - 65 Street*

Dear Sirs:

With regard to the above mentioned listing, this is your authority to advise all co-operative members of the Edmonton Real Estate Board Co-operative Listing Bureau of the following:

Listing Sold for $ *13,700.00*   by *Howatt, Perry & Burton Ltd*

Listing Expired _____ 19 _____

Listing Renewed to _____ 19 _____

Price Reduction—Remarks, Etc.

RECEIVED
AUG 12 1952

Broker *L. Winterburn & Son*
Date *August 11* 19 *52*   Address *H.C. Agency Bldg by Brady*

Listing Bureau Ltd. after amalgamation was held in the ballroom at Hotel Macdonald on May 27, 1959. This amalgamation did not involve the creation of a new organization. The Edmonton Real Estate Board Co-operative Listing Bureau Ltd. carried on as the flag ship for organized real estate in Edmonton.

Growth of the Co-op

Once the Edmonton Real Estate Board Co-operative Listing Bureau had been established, the next challenge was promoting its use by the various real estate companies. Norm Winterburn also played a very important role in this campaign. He made presentations to the sales staff of various companies. He encouraged their participation by pointing out that the multiple listing service would allow a salesman to have a listing circulated to other members. It also helped smaller companies with a small staff and few or no branch offices to build up a clientele.

Norm was also involved in the organization of social events. The philosophy behind these activities was to encourage camaraderie amongst members of the real estate industry. These events included charter trips to Las Vegas and Spain. He also organized events in Edmonton that featured his expertise as a magician.

Despite some initial opposition, the co-op became an established institution in the industry through the efforts of Norm Winterburn and others. The first property listing of the Edmonton Real Estate Board Co-operative Listing Bureau was received on August 7, 1952, for a house located at 11158 - 65 Street in the Highlands. Norm Winterburn had the first listing and also sold the first house through the Co-operative Listing Bureau. By September 23, 1952, they had 177 listings. By then the Bureau had sold twenty-five properties with a total value of $241,200.00. The value would continue to increase every year thereafter until 1982.

Permanent staff

The size and activities of the Board, particularly after amalgamation in 1959,

justified the hiring of full-time staff to handle its day-to-day activities.

The first employee of the Multiple Listing Bureau was Grace Forbes. She was the secretary and manager of Elmore Pointer's insurance business, which was located in the Wallace Building. When the Multiple Listing Bureau took over Pointer's office, Grace Forbes was hired to manage the daily activities of the Bureau.

The daily operations of the Bureau when it began involved the preparation of the *Daily Bulletin*. Initially, the Co-operative Listing Bureau contracted out the photography of the buildings to McDermid Studios while the Co-operative Listing Bureau prepared information cards on the property. When the photographs were received they were attached to the information cards and copied for distribution to the membership.

Delays in obtaining the photographs from McDermids ended when Gordon Whiddon was hired on January 1, 1957. His duties at that time consisted of photographing the new listings in the morning and typing the listing information onto paper stencils in the afternoon. It was Whiddon's responsibility to run off the *Daily Bulletin* on the Gestetner using tear sheets, which preceded the current catalogue's style.

Tony Hamilton is a thirty-year veteran of the Production Department. When she joined the Board on July 15, 1966 Tony's first duties with the Board involved the preparation and printing of the *Daily Bulletin* on a Gestetner machine. She also assisted Gordon in the preparation of the plates used to produce the listing sheets. With the move to the building on 142nd Street, she became part of the pro-

Grace Forbes was the first employee of the Board, seen here at work in the Wallace Building.
(Edmonton Real Estate Board)

Tony Hamilton handled the production needs of the EREB for over thirty years.
(Edmonton Real Estate Board)

Gordon Whiddon (far left) and other staff members celebrate the official opening of the new EREB building on Princess Elizabeth Avenue on November 30, 1962.
(Edmonton Real Estate Board)

Kelly Haugen served as executive secretary from September 1, 1959 to March 31, 1976.

(Edmonton Real Estate Board)

The Wallace Building was the location of the first permanent office of the Edmonton Real Estate Board. It was located where the Westin Hotel parkade is today.

(Edmonton Real Estate Board)

duction department which is responsible for the printing of the Board's publications such as the *Daily Bulletin* and a weekly newsletter. The production department now uses the most advanced press to meet the needs of the Board.

In 1959 Kelly Haugen became executive secretary following the death of Henry Flewwelling. Kelly Haugen was born in Grand Forks, North Dakota, in 1910 but his family moved to Canada when he was six weeks old. After graduating from Camrose College and the University of Minnesota he joined the RCAF in 1940. He was discharged with the rank of Squadron Leader on October 1946. After World War Two he worked for the Soldier Settlement Board of Canada, helping to resettle veterans on land. In 1955 he left government service and sold real estate in Edmonton for Alex McCrae and Administration and Trust. Kelly Haugen served as executive secretary from September 1, 1959, to March 31, 1976, when he retired from the Board.

Norm Winterburn had been president of the Board in 1972 and 1973. On April 4, 1974, he was hired as assistant to Kelly Haugen until Kelly retired on March 31, 1976. He was the executive vice-president of the Edmonton Board until March 31, 1982. During his term he introduced a pension plan for EREB staff.

Another past-president who joined the Board as an employee was Max Kaplan, who had served as president in 1967 and 1968. He was assistant to Norm Winterburn from 1976 to 1982. He played a major role in supervising the construction of the building on 142nd Street.

Permanent offices

Along with a permanent staff came permanent offices. The Edmonton Real Estate Board had traditionally met in the offices of its members or at the Edmonton Chamber of Commerce. When the Edmonton Real Estate Board Co-operative Listing Bureau moved into suite 304 of the Wallace building at 9921 - 101A Avenue in 1952, it would remain there for six years. In 1955 the Edmonton Real Estate Board also moved into the Wallace building, with the Edmonton Real Estate Board Co-operative Listing Bureau providing secretarial services.

In 1958 the Co-operative Listing Bureau and the Edmonton Real Estate Board moved to the Brown Building at 9107 - 118 Avenue, where they remained until 1962. From 1962 to 1979 the Edmonton Real Estate Board occupied a new building at 10505 Princess Elizabeth Ave, built at a cost of $50,000.

The move to the building on Princess Elizabeth Avenue in 1962 had a significant effect on the day-to-day operations of the Board. Gordon Whidden got an assistant and a process lab, which ended dependence on outside services. The Edmonton Real Estate Board Co-operative Listing Bureau now had its own printing plant and mailing department on the lower floor, its own darkroom, and the necessary camera equipment for photographing properties offered for sale. The Board was able to provide full details and photographs of any property within forty-eight hours of its being listed to more than 400 sales agents throughout the city. Initial notice of the listing was provided in the *Daily Bulletin*.

The premier event in the history of the Edmonton Real Estate Board offices was the building of its new premises on 142 Street and 112 Avenue. The site chosen was the former location of a Second World War American military installation. It was purchased for $700,000, which was the selling price for the old building on Princess Elizabeth Avenue. Recommendations for the design of the building came from real estate boards across Canada and United States, with many ideas from local members. Cec Cunningham, Graham Downey, and Jim Baker each served consecutively as chairman of the committee coordinating the construction of the building. The architect was James Wensley. Plans were completed on February 1979 and the building was officially opened in June 1981 at a cost of $4,095,676, which included both land and building.

The result is one of the best facilities for a Real Estate Board in Canada. The building has

sales representatives.

In August 1979, work began on the computerization of the MLS® functions. There-after, statistics could be compiled quickly and accurately. The first computerized *Daily Bulletin* was produced by December. By April 1980 accounts receivable had been entered on the computer system. Norm Bulat became the manager of the new computer systems department.

Standing committees

The construction of the new premises and the creation of a permanent staff to take over day-to-day duties did not eliminate the need of the standing committee system. These committees continued to provide the leadership for the Board's activities.

The Legislation Committee continued to review the Real Estate Agents' Licensing Act.

space for all aspects of its operations along with a parkade. Printing of all regular Board publications except the catalogue and the *Real Estate Weekly* is carried out onsite. Meeting rooms and a 200 seat auditorium accommodate committee meetings and educational programs. The new building on 142 Street was also designed to facilitate the upgrading of its computer system.

Expansion of services

The new services included a catalogue introduced in January of 1973 to replace the daily perforated listing sheets. In 1978 the board of directors decided that computerization should play an important role in the operations of the Board. Bill Colman of Colman Organ and Co. was retained as a computer consultant. Computerization of operations began in July 1979 when the membership department converted all of their records. This enabled the Board to produce mailing labels, to update the membership roster quickly, and to provide immediate answers to inquiries regarding the status of agents and

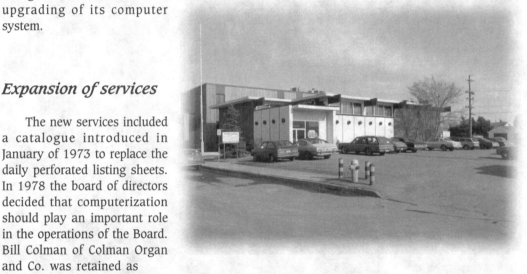

The committee also monitored other legislation by the federal and provincial governments. The federal proposals to amend the Combines Investigation Act in 1975 was of particular concern, because the MLS® system could be considered a restraint to trade. The revisions, it was feared, would end organized real estate and the MLS® system as they had operated up to then. Another proposed change was that infractions of the law were to be dealt with under the criminal code.

Advising all three levels of government on policies and procedures related to the real estate industry was another task of the Legislation Committee. Local concerns included having the city pay commissions to real estate agents who sold city-owned industrial or commercial land. In February 1960 city council voted to pay a commission of three percent of the selling price of the land. The commission would be sent to the Real Estate Board, which would distribute it to the agent who sold the land. Alderman Ed Leger, chairman of the city council's special committee on land sales, said distribution through the Real Estate Board would prevent city involvement in disputes among agents, and would establish better liaisons between real estate agents and clients who arrived in Edmonton to look for industrial or commercial sites.

The Membership Committee, which had struggled since 1927 to expand the membership, now had to adjust to sustained increases in membership. Between 1951 and 1980, membership went from 61 to a high of 3,356. This acceleration in membership was evident as early as January 14, 1952, when nineteen new members were admitted at one meeting. At the meeting of June 25, 1957, 103 new members were approved, thus setting a record for the number of new members admitted at one time. This increase in membership resulted from the cooperation of companies such as Melton Real Estate and Weber Brothers, who enrolled their sales representatives en masse in the Board.

Despite increased membership the committee launched a membership drive. In January 1952 the committee received a list of agents from the office of the superintendent of insurance. Once informed of the value of the services offered by the Board, few members of the industry needed much encouragement to join.

With the problem of attracting new members solved, this committee had the ongoing responsibility of scrutinizing new membership applications.

Members of the Edmonton Real Estate Board met at the old Seven Seas Restaurant in June of 1955.
(Edmonton Real Estate Board)

Ethics have always been an important part of the Edmonton Real Estate Board since they were at the heart of its efforts to ensure the self-policing of the industry and to improve its image. The importance of this issue is evident in the adoption of a Code of Ethics in 1927, in the efforts to obtain legislation, and in the Board's cooperation with government to ensure its enforcement. Up until 1953 ethics and arbitration were handled by one committee. The Ethics Committee continued to arbitrate the problems of the members as long as no commission was involved. (The least active committee, much to everyone's satisfaction, was the Arbitration Committee. It dealt with any commission disputes.) The lack of meetings reflected the informal network amongst the agents and sales representatives that effectively dealt with concerns before they got to the arbitration stage. The Ethics Committee was also not overworked for the same reason.

One of the activities of the Ethics Committee in the early 1950s was to supervise the pledging ceremony. The pledge was a commitment by the member to abide by the bylaws and code of ethics of the Association. It was also a commitment to make *"every reasonable effort to avoid controversies."* If arbitration became necessary, the members pledged to abide by the Arbitration Committee's decision. The final part of the pledge was to abide by the rule *"do unto others as we would have others do unto us."* The first pledge ceremony was conducted by Mark Cummings on January 29, 1954. The idea of the pledge went back to 1927 and would continue until the late 1950s when it was dropped.

Publicity initiatives became important in the golden age. The Edmonton Real Estate Association had functioned without most Edmonton residents knowing of its existence. The Edmonton Real Estate Board Co-operative Listing Bureau therefore made a deliberate effort to raise the profile of the Board in the community. Advertisements on Edmonton Transit System buses, billboards, and business cards started the process. The billboard advertisements were on the Scona Bend Apartments building and on a second building located at the corner of 124th Street and 118th Avenue. The Bureau also advertised in newspapers and on radio. The Board sponsored the telecasts by Bryan Hall of Edmonton Eskimo games.

A committee concerning acreages, farms, and recreation properties was the last to be created during the golden age. From the start one of its main goals has been to educate other agents and sale representatives of the special needs of this kind of property. The committee was able to give this market more

exposure by having special sections in the catalogue and special information fields for the computer listings.

A monthly publication had never been undertaken by the Association because of lack of funds and its small size. The rapid growth in membership meant that some type of publication needed to be developed. The result was the *Edmonton Realtor*, which began in March 1960.

As Dennis Stewart in his presidential greeting observed,

Promoting the activities of the Board in the 1960s.
(Edmonton Real Estate Board)

For many years our Association (had) been without any means of officially

Public display showing the progress of the Board and promoting its activities in 1962.
(Edmonton Real Estate Board)

sponsor two, two-day educational courses to be held in May. CREA required a guarantee of at least twenty candidates for each course. Each candidate would pay $15 per course. Since each course would be full at thirty candidates, it was decided to admit applicants on a first-come, first-served basis. The first course was very successful.

Given the growing demand for education, an Education Committee was established in 1952. This committee implemented an education program in 1956 when the Board started a "primary school" for new members of the industry. This course provided an introduction to such topics as sales-manship, appraisal, law, brokerage, and ethics.

The primary school made the Edmonton Real Estate Board a leader in the formal education of its members. Requests came from across Canada for copies of the *Primary School Manual.* The Education Committee responded by assembling detailed lectures for such a manual. The ongoing organization and operation of the primary schools would continue to be the Education Committee's main function for most of the golden age.

In 1970 the committee began to expand the educational program to include seminars. In the spring of 1970 a successful eight-week salesman course attracted 402 attendants. In 1971 an all-day sales seminar featuring a popular American motivational speaker, Douglas Edwards, was held. Four sales training films were purchased for use by the members.

Consistent with the Board's interest in education, the suggestion was made in May 1952 that it establish a library, but the shortage of space in the Brown Building was a problem. Given this situation, the committee decided to concentrate its efforts on collecting books for a library to be opened when space was found. Space for a library was resolved when the building was built on Princess Elizabeth Avenue. Library facilities were improved even further with the construction of

communicating with its members. The "Edmonton Realtor" will be the official voice of over 500 members of the real estate fraternity in Edmonton. This publication will prove to be a milestone on the road to success of organized real estate in Edmonton.

To build a strong association everyone must be informed. We want the Edmonton Real Estate Board to be the strongest body of organized REALTORS in Canada. To do this we must be constantly on the alert for methods and means of improving ourselves, our business and our Association.

With only one minor change in format, it would continue to be published until September 1961. It was followed in 1978 by the *MLS® Informer*, a bimonthly publication edited by Art Jones. It included articles by presidents on traditional themes such as the growth of the Board, ethics, and education. It provided a list of top sales representatives, new additions for the library, upcoming events, and announcements concerning educational programs.

In March 1952, CREA advised the Edmonton Real Estate Board that it would the present building. The library acquires not only printed material but also audio tapes and video tapes for training purposes.

Since 1927 the Edmonton Real Estate Board had been organized on a two-system format based on agents and salesmen. During 1952-1981 far more salesmen joined than agents, and "salesladies" also entered the industry. The creation of the Salesmen's Committee in 1960 was a way of dealing with this growth. Unlike other committees, it elected its own chairperson and its own members to the board of directors.

The Salesmen's Committee dealt with the special needs and interests of the sales representatives. The committee had members on the board of directors, which gave the sales representatives an opportunity to bring their issues to the Board, such as Sunday open houses, a group insurance plan, and part-time sales people. The committee also organized seminars of interest to the members.

Managing the Board's multiple listing service was the responsibility of the Photo Listing Committee. The MLS® was particularly critical to the Board since the fees from this service provided the funds for the operation of the Board. The committee encouraged the use of the system and worked towards making improvements. Contests between the sales staff for the highest total over a certain period helped to promote its use. Improvements involved buying new machinery for producing the *Daily Bulletin*.

Social life

During the golden age, the entertainment activities of the Board expanded beyond the program of guest speakers and musical presentations, and became independent of the regular meetings of the membership. Organizing social activities was the responsibility of the Program and Attendance Committee. The Program and Attendance Committee's first organized event was a bowling league started on September 9, 1960, at the B and B Lanes.

Social activities had been part of the Association's history since 1933 when the first golf tournament was held at the Prince Rupert Golf Club. The April 1960 issue of *The Edmonton Realtor* suggested that a golf tournament would be the appropriate recreational activity for the summer.

Other social athletic activities included an annual curling bonspiel and a softball league. By 1979 curling had become so popular that only members were allowed to participate. The curling bonspiel was held in conjunction with another popular event: the "smoker." The annual trap shooting contest reflected the influence of Ed Shaske, who won nine Canadian Championships and was on the 1968 Canadian Olympic team. He was also instrumental in organizing the facilities for the 1978 Commonwealth Games. He served as president of the EREB in 1965 and 1966. Ed is also a Life Member.

Social activities were very popular in the Board's history. At this time no individual company parties were held and the Board organized all activities. There was real camaraderie since it was a small group and there was less movement between companies. One popular contributor to the social life of the Board was Howie Molstad's band.

REALTORS join in Klondike Days festivities.
(Edmonton Real Estate Board)

Recognition system

Formal recognition of the accomplishments of members of the Edmonton Real Estate Board was another innovation of the golden age. The first recognition awards were given in 1953, when Andy Whyte, Lou Weber, and Luke Winterburn were made Honorary Members. Shortly thereafter Sam Ferris and H. Milton Martin were similarly honored.

The presentation of these awards was an opportunity for the veterans of the industry in Edmonton to pass on some advice to the rapidly increasing number of new members. Sam Ferris advised the members that: *"If you really take this business in the right spirit and you set yourselves to it you will find the same as I have found, and you will find the same as many other men before you who have arrived in this business — it is the finest business in the world, and there is not a business in the world where you can make more money by good management, sound investments and carry on, never get discouraged — if you do, you're sunk — Don't worry about the deal you lost but go right on as if you had never been working on that deal. If you have the right spirit, the right ability, just as soon as that one goes you see another one pop up on the horizon and away you go."*

After 1953 the honorary membership award evolved into one given to non-members of the Edmonton Real Estate Board who have rendered outstanding service to the real estate industry.

During the golden age the Board also began to award Life Memberships. This award was for outstanding service to the industry but the recipient had to be a member of the Edmonton Real Estate Board.

Life Members have all the rights and privileges of membership and are not required to pay membership dues. They cannot, however, hold office or vote at meetings unless they are a regular member of the Board with such privileges. (Recipients of life memberships are listed in an appendix.)

The Board also recognized the current successes of its members with its salesman contest begun in March 1960. Points were credited to a member when he or she sold a house through the MLS® system. The prizes ranged from a free lunch to $500. The monthly winners were also seated at a special table at general meetings as further recognition of their achievements.

Million Dollar Sales Club

In 1967 the directors of the Edmonton Real Estate Board approved the formation of a "club" to be known as the Million Dollar Sales Club. The qualifications for membership then was the accumulation of $1 million in sales "points" in three consecutive calendar years. Points equated to the dollar value of the selling price of a home. Thus, if a home sold for $40,000, then the listing and the sales broker were each awarded 20,000 points. The amount was set to be achieved at a time when the average sale price of residential property was approximately $16,000. The first club member was Fred Kurylo.

As land values went up, the qualifying time period was decreased, eventually to one year by 1976. In 1978 procedures were revised further. A formula was prepared to maintain the level of difficulty regardless of market conditions. The formula involved dividing the average residential sale price of the past year by the average residential selling price of 1975 (established as the base year) and multiplying the result by one million. Using this formula the qualifying amount reached $1,591,000 by 1979, $1,801,000 by 1985 and $2,556,000 by 1995.

In 1980, the directors established a Five Million Dollar Sales Club, and a Ten Million Dollar Sales Club effective in 1981. The qualifying volume for both clubs was fixed at five and ten million points.

Men & women builders of the Board

The members of the EREB in the 1950s were an interesting mix of people. It included veterans of the industry who had been involved since 1907. This older generation was represented by H. M. E. Evans and H. Milton Martin. Both men had been part of the Edmonton land boom pre-1918 and the Edmonton Real Estate Exchange in 1909. Both Martin and Evans were from the era when real estate was sold by an agency that also sold insurance. Martin died in 1962 at the age of 90. Evans passed away at the age of 97 in 1973.

By the 1950s, a second generation of Edmontonians had followed their fathers into the industry. This group of dynamic young leaders in the industry included Norm Winterburn, whose contributions to the establishment and growth of the Board have already been noted. He was the son of Luke Winterburn. Norm was born in 1920 and

Norm Winterburn played a key role in launching a multiple listing service in Edmonton.
(Edmonton Real Estate Board)

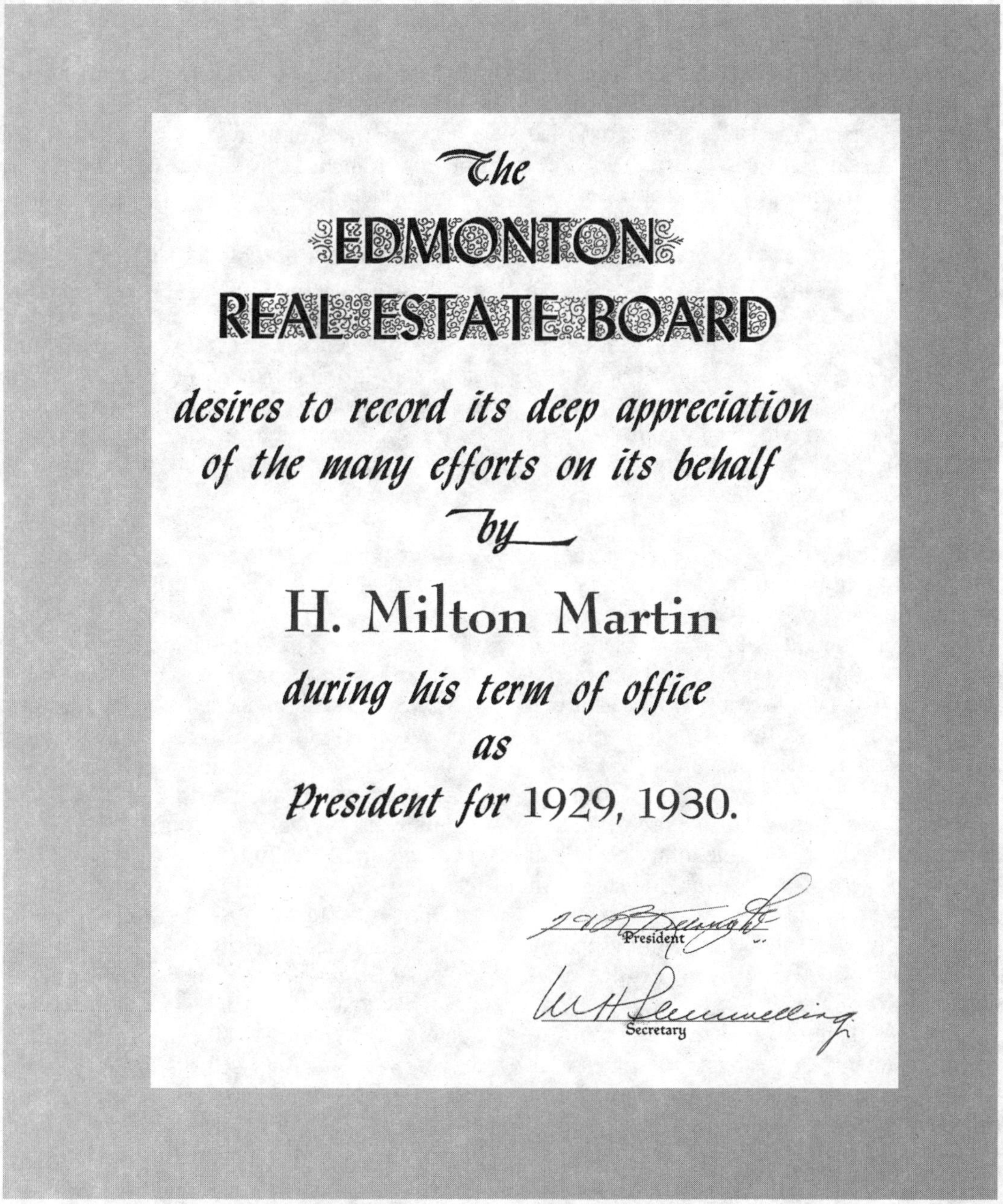

The
EDMONTON
REAL ESTATE BOARD
desires to record its deep appreciation
of the many efforts on its behalf
by
H. Milton Martin
during his term of office
as
President for 1929, 1930.

President

Secretary

H. Milton Martin was recognized for his significant contributions to the Edmonton Real Estate Board
(Edmonton Real Estate Board)

educated in Edmonton. In 1938 he joined his father's real estate firm. He recalls that his first major purchase was a house costing $1,100. He put $200 down and had payments of $25 per month, plus $2.50 per month taxes. He then rented it for $27.50 per month.

In 1942, Norm joined the Royal Canadian Navy and after serving on the high seas, worked at King's College in Halifax. He received his discharge in August 1945 and returned to real estate, to become the agent of his father's firm. His presidency of the Edmonton Real Estate Board in 1950 began a long and distinguished career dedicated to the development of organized real estate in Edmonton. He also served on the board of directors of AREA and CREA. For his many contributions he was awarded a Life Membership from the EREB.

Another member of this second generation was Howie Molstad. Born in Edmonton in 1919, he was educated in Edmonton where he completed one year at the University of Alberta. He joined the RCAF in 1942 and served until 1946. Upon being discharged he joined his father's firm, Molstad and Co. Ltd., which was founded in 1910, and later became president. He and his father branched out and had four offices with a staff of about fifty. Between 1951 and 1953 Howie and his father

Stan Melton stressed the importance of good customer and employee relations.
(Edmonton Real Estate Board)

Stan Melton (left) President of Melton Real Estate, receives top Edmonton Real Estate Board 1963 Sales Production Award from Ray Buxton, retiring president of the Edmonton Real Estate Board. Melton Real Estate achieved this award in recording sales totalling $4,172,290.00 during 1963.
(Edmonton Real Estate Board)

established a series of finance companies. The first was the Star Finance Co., which provided mortgage loans. Howie's many contributions to the Edmonton Real Estate Board included his term as president in 1957. He was awarded a Life Membership in 1985.

An important part of the Molstad organization has been Howie Molstad's wife, Cora. She received a Life Membership in 1994. The real estate tradition in the Molstad family is being carried on by their son, Rick. With Rick as part of the firm, Molstad Real Estate continues to be Edmonton's oldest surviving real estate company.

A third veteran with family connections to the Edmonton real estate industry was Darrell Ball. His career in the mercantile business was interrupted by World War Two, when he served in the Canadian Navy. After his discharge he returned to the mercantile business before starting his own firm in 1953. He was assisted by his father, Frank Ball. Frank had been a real estate salesman specializing in commercial property, particularly hotels. Darrell was active on a number of committees and was given a Life Membership in the Edmonton Real Estate Board.

Melton Real Estate was one of the stars of the golden age because of the influence of Stan Melton, who was also a veteran and son of an Edmonton real estate saleman. The founder of the company was his father, Louis Timothy Melton, who was born in France and immigrated to Canada in 1887.

In 1918 Timothy moved to Edmonton, where he entered the real estate business. He was employed by Allan, Celom, McKay and Greene for the next four years, then started his own business. He opened the Stanley Investment Co., which was officially incorporated on March 10, 1925. After 1932 the name of the company was changed to L. T. Melton Realty. The company specialized in west-end properties, since Tim's motto was: *"Buy land in the west end of*

a growing city, keep it and it will keep you".

Stan Melton took over the company after he returned from the war. Under Stan's direction the company quickly expanded, opening branches throughout Edmonton and western Canada. He used existing personnel trained in Melton policy and ethics. Melton Real Estate was one of the first real estate companies in Edmonton to establish branch offices in residential districts. These offices were convenient for the customer and placed sales staff in the community where they could become familiar with the area and its residents. In 1955 the company expanded to Calgary. Its success was based on good customer and employee relations.

The company also coined one of the most familiar advertising slogans in Edmonton's history, *"call a Melton man and start packing."*

The system of branch offices was an important part of Stan's concept of how sales staff acquired listings. In his view, a sales representative without listings was a merchant with nothing to sell. A listing was the purpose, reason, and justification for a merchant being in business. To obtain listings Stan Melton recommended finding those people with a reason to sell.

In 1968 Melton Real Estate became a public company when it was listed on the Toronto Stock Exchange. Following Stan Melton's death from a heart attack at an Edmonton Eskimo football game in 1973, the decision was made to sell off the real estate brokerage part of the business to A. E. LePage of Toronto. The company then concentrated on land development, housing construction, and income properties development as Melcor Developments Ltd. Stan's son Tim was president.

Stan served as president of the EREB in 1954, as president of AREA in 1955, and as president of CREA in 1963. AREA and CREA each awarded him a Life Membership in recognition of his outstanding service to the industry.

Contributions to the operation of the Board by other members of the Melton organization were made by Mark Dubord, Ed Sande, Ian McKinnon, Garf Bennett, Dave Crawford, Murray Beckhusan, Harold Dundas, and Don Clark. These people either began their real estate careers with Melton or were long-term employees who remained with the company even after its purchase by A. E. LePage.

Mark Dubord started with Melton Real Estate in 1950. After leaving Melton Real Estate, he operated his own company with the exception of an interlude with Royal Trust. His contributions to the Board began in the 1960s, when he served on a variety of committees

committee work, he received a Life Membership in 1994.

In 1959, Garf Bennett started with Melton Real Estate. He established his own company in 1976. Garf was president of AREA in 1977 and served as a director of CREA in 1978. He was made a Life Member of the Edmonton Real Estate Board in 1988.

The ongoing commitment of volunteers ensured the growth of the Edmonton Real Estate Board. Back row left to right:
Neis Greidanius, Graham Downey, Norm Winterburn, Herman King, Don Helmers, Ted Dale, Mark Dubord, Stan Melton, Chris Graefe
Seated left to right:
Max Kaplan, Ed Shaske
(Edmonton Real Estate Board)

including public relations. He was a director for many years and was president in 1969. He was awarded a Life Membership.

Another "Melton Man" who started his own company is Ed Sande. He worked for Melton Real Estate from 1955 until 1963 before going into business for himself. He served on many committees, including the Professional Standards Committee, and received a Life Membership from the Board.

Ian McKinnon played an important role in the expansion of Melton Real Estate. In 1970 he established the Winnipeg branch where he remained as regional manager. Upon his return to Edmonton in 1975, he established his own company. In recognition of his work for the Board, which included extensive

After working for Melton Real Estate from 1968 to 1972, Dave Crawford joined Don Spencer as a partner in Spencer Real Estate. Since 1979 he has been sole owner. He served as president of EREB in 1986 and as president of AREA in 1990/91. He was named REALTOR of the Year in 1984 and received a Life Membership from the EREB in 1992.

Melton employed Murray Beckhuson from 1948 to 1978. He rose from salesman to become a company director. Murray served as president of the Edmonton Real Estate Board in 1958 and was awarded a Life Membership in 1989.

A builder of the Board who was also a long service member of Melton Real Estate is Harold Dundas. He was born in Onoway, where his family farmed until he was ten. The family then moved to Fort Saskatchewan. Harold moved to Edmonton in 1959 to begin his career in real estate. He started with a small firm called Keystone Agencies, eventually becoming vice-president and divisional general manager for Royal LePage. As with many Board members who came into the industry in the golden age, he considers the greater emphasis on education and training in the 1980s as one of the more important developments in the industry. He was president of the Board in 1975 and was awarded a Life Membership in 1987.

Don Clark began his career with Melton Real Estate in 1963. He remained with the company after its acquisition by A. E. LePage. He served as president of the EREB in 1984 and has been active in the Realtors' Charitable Foundation. In recognition of his service Don was awarded a Life Membership in 1991.

Jack Weber was a major architect of the Edmonton Real Estate Board.
(Edmonton Real Estate Board)

Another outstanding figure in the Edmonton real estate business who followed his father into the industry was Jack Weber. He began his real estate career with his father and uncle's firm, Weber Brothers, in 1939, working as a collection clerk. Later he became secretary-treasurer. In 1945 he purchased the shares of the Edmonton Credit Co. and took over control of the family firm. Like Melton, Weber Brothers expanded after the Second World War. Branch offices were established in order to compete with their most serious competitor, Melton Real Estate. Weber Brothers established offices in other areas in Alberta. The firm was sold to a group of senior employees in 1979.

A very active community booster, Jack's efforts ranged from encouraging investment in the western Canadian economy to promoting Klondike Days. He was one of the original "Six Sleepy Sourdoughs" who launched Klondike Days. In recognition of his role he was awarded the Cheechako Award in 1975 by the Canadian Progress Club and received the key to the City of Edmonton the following year. He also served as president of both the Edmonton and Alberta Chamber of Commerce, was northern Alberta CNIB district president, and in 1949 served as president of the Boyle Street Community League.

Like so many other individuals of his day, Jack Weber divided his time between his business and his work in the various real estate associations. He became president of the Edmonton Real Estate Board in 1953 after having served as secretary-treasurer. While secretary-treasurer he introduced the practice of preparing audited statements for the Association. In his 1953 president's report, he cited the need for education and the need for a permanent secretary. Since earlier suggestions for revising the licensing act had involved the need for education, the Licensing Committee became the Licensing and Education Committee. It included Don Spencer, Stan Melton, and Dennis Stewart. Their efforts resulted in an educational course being offered through the University of Alberta Department of Extension leading to FRI (Fellow of the Real Estate Institute) and/or AACI (Acredited Appraiser, Canadian Institute) designations.

Jack's strong attachment to education was evident in his president's report in which he encouraged older members of the Association to take the course: "*It is true that with their long experience in the Real Estate Business, they have, perhaps, little need of taking an Education Course, which, in many respects, is quite elementary, but I do sincerely feel that if those who have been in the business for a number of years lead the way by taking the course, whether they feel they need it or not, it will provide the spark and incentive for the newer members of our profession to do likewise.*"

After serving as president of AREA in 1953, Jack Weber went on to become president of CREA. He was also a founding member and the first president of the Canadian Institute of Realtors (CIR). He helped found and later served as president of the International Real Estate Association (FIABCI). The City of Paris awarded him the Silver Medal in recognition of his efforts to establish this organization. He suffered a severe stroke in 1975, which forced him to be hospitalized until his death in 1989. He was made a Life Member of the EREB.

Another member of the Weber Brothers organization who was also president of the Board in 1980 was Al Scott. He was one of the senior executives who took over Weber Brothers following Jack's retirement.

Homer Kellough was as involved in the EREB as Melton and Weber. He began his real estate career in 1945 when he became sales manager for William Hawkeye, who operated a real estate and insurance company in Edmonton. He became a partner the following year. In 1948 he joined Weber Brothers as a sales representative. By 1951 he was manager of the real estate division. He left Weber Brothers in 1955 to establish the firm of Kellough and Haliburton in partnership with Jack Haliburton. It continued until 1958. After serving as president and managing director of the firm of Trotter, McIntyre and Kellough for one year, he took over the firm, renaming it H. R. Kellough Realty Ltd., which he operated until his death in 1971. He had branch offices similar to the Weber Brothers and Melton Real Estate. Homer was one of the first of the established firms to hire women. Doris Woodward managed his west end office. He is remembered as an individual who inspired loyalty, who worked with his employees to improve their performance, and who encouraged education. He was a strong supporter of the cooperative approach to real estate. In recognition of this fact he received a Life Membership.

The Kellough organization supplied its share of people who contributed to the development of the Board. Norm Murray began his real estate career in 1951 when an accident prevented him from continuing his farming and pipeline construction work. He started with a small company called Leader Realty. He eventually moved to Weber Bros. Realty and then to Trotter, McIntyre, and Kellough, where he remained until 1971. After three years as a partner in the firm of Kellough Realty, he established his own company, Norm Murray Realty.

Norm made significant contributions to organized real estate both locally and provincially. He served eighteen years as a director of either the EREB or AREA. He was president of the EREB in 1976 and AREA in 1986/87. He received a Life Membership in 1986.

Veterans who had no prior experience in the real estate industry also contributed to its vitality during the golden age. After serving in the Army for three-and-one half years and then obtaining a bachelor's degree from the Faculty of Commerce, Dennis Stewart began his career as a real estate agent. He left real estate

Jack Weber was one of the original "Six Sleepy Sourdoughs" who launched Klondike Days in Edmonton in 1962.
(Edmonton Real Estate Board)

between 1954 and 1956 to organize First Investors Corporation, but he returned later and became president and agent representing Imperial Real Estate Ltd. Imperial Real Estate Ltd. was a large company that was active in all aspects of the industry. He served as the president of CREA in 1969.

Upon graduating from high school in Edmonton, Don Spencer spent four years with a wholesale firm and five years as a life underwriter. His service overseas during World War Two was with the RCAF, in which he reached the rank of flying officer. After the war Don worked for a year as a sales representative with Chapman Agencies. In 1948, he formed a partnership known as Spencer and Grierson Ltd. that lasted for twelve years. He then established his own firm, known as D. M. Spencer Agencies Ltd. He served as the president of the EREB in 1951, and AREA in 1957. He was made a Life Member of the EREB.

Other new recruits to the Edmonton real estate industry came from rural Alberta or small towns in central and northern Alberta. They were attracted to Edmonton because of improved employment opportunities. Earl

Pottage, Ray Buxton, and Barry Gogal are three people who made a successful transition to the big city.

Earl Pottage grew up on a farm in the Sedgewick area and graduated from high school in Camrose. (A fellow student was Al Larson, an executive secretary of AREA.) Earl began his career in real estate in 1964 with McBeth Agencies, eventually establishing his own company in 1969 in partnership with Pat Burns. In 1980 he bought Pat out and in 1984 changed the name of the company to Pottage Realty.

Earl's involvement in the activities of the EREB reflects the influence of his first boss, Frank Oakie. Frank encouraged Earl to take the real estate programs leading to his FRI designation. Because Earl attained the highest mark recorded for the entrance exam for both salesperson and agent, he was approached to become involved with the Education Committee of both the Edmonton Real Estate Board and AREA. He has also served as a director of both organizations. He received a Life Membership in the EREB in 1988 and another from AREA. Earl was president of AREA in 1979/80.

After selling his garage in Fairview in 1955, Ray Buxton moved to Edmonton to begin a new business career. He spent three years with Imperial Real Estate before starting his own company in 1958. Buxton Real Estate grew to twelve offices in Edmonton and Calgary with 130 employees. Ray sold his interests in the company in 1976 and formed Javelin Real Estate, which specialized in commercial and industrial properties.

After serving as president of the Edmonton Real Estate Board in 1962 and 1963, he went on to become president of AREA in 1972 and CREA in 1982. A strong supporter of education in the industry, Ray recalls that when he entered the field there were no educational programs for salespeople. He had to find his own books, periodicals, and university courses on the subject of real estate. In his view: *"the most important thing that organized real estate has done is recognize the necessity of educating salespeople. It's extremely important to the growth of the industry."* This emphasis on education fulfils, in his view, the original purpose of real estate boards, rather than the operation of an MLS® service.

Active participation was the key to the on-going success of the association. EREB members included back row left to right: George Stott, Stan Melton, Dennis Stewart, Norm Winterburn, Homer Kellough. Front row left to right: Howie Molstad, Mark Cummings, Murray Beckhuson.
(Edmonton Real Estate Board)

Real estate attracted Barry Gogal at a very young age to his very successful business career. In 1971, at the age of 21, he became a salesman for Borden Real Estate. He remained with the company after its purchase by Royal Trust. In 1975 he left Royal Trust to establish Gogal Real Estate Ltd. He also shifted his activities to commercial properties. From 1982 to 1988 he held senior positions with Canada Trust. Since 1988 he has been a partner in Western Realty Group, which specializes in industrial, commercial and investment (IC&I) property.

Barry has been involved in all three levels of organized real estate. His contributions began in 1977, when he served on the Membership Committee of the Edmonton Real Estate Board. He became president of the Board in 1981, and of AREA in 1985. His participation in CREA began in 1986 when he became a director. He has received Life Memberships from all three organizations. He was REALTOR of the Year in 1986.

Native Edmontonians also entered the real estate business in large numbers. One important builder of the Board from this group was Graham Downey, who started his real estate career in 1960 when he was employed by Royal Realty. Later he worked for Melton Real Estate. He then spent four years at Royal Trust, where he specialized in residential and industrial sales.

When Canada Permanent Trust expanded their operations into Alberta in 1966, Graham was asked to oversee the start of a branch in Edmonton. He set up the first office and worked as district manager for the company for the next fourteen years. Since 1982 he has run his own company called Downey and Associates.

Graham has served on the Edmonton Real Estate Board in many capacities since the 1960s. He has been a director and was president in 1978. He has also served on many committees, beginning with the Ethics and Business Practices Committee (formerly known as the Ethics and Arbitration Committee).

His service to the industry also includes being president of AREA in 1974 and serving as Alberta director of CREA. He has received Life Memberships from both AREA and CREA. He is also a past president of the Realtors Charitable Foundation. Graham was REALTOR of the Year in 1989.

Before the golden age, the real estate in-

dustry in Edmonton had been an exclusively male occupation. Women had served as secretaries but not as sales people, branch managers, or directors of the Edmonton Real Estate Association. A number of pioneers changed this situation. Kitty Callaghen, Jessie Oxford-Spencer, Mabel Gordon, Ruth Thatcher, and Connie Kennedy were the first women to enter this male bastion of Edmonton business.

After successfully completing the real estate primary school in October of 1960, Jessie Oxford-Spencer pursued a career in real estate with Weber Brothers, eventually becoming the manager of the central west branch of that company.

One of the first real estate sales women in Winnipeg was Mabel Gordon. She began her real estate career in 1956. In 1965 Mabel moved to Edmonton where she was involved in various community activities until 1972, when she went back to selling real estate. In 1976 Mabel became a member of the Million Dollar Sales Club. From 1979 to 1984 she served as the first woman on the board of directors for the EREB. In 1985 she was made a Life Member, the first woman to gain that distinction.

Montreal was where Ruth Thatcher began her career in real estate. One problem she encountered when she moved to Edmonton was having to deal with an executive who initially refused to accompany her to look at homes because she was a woman. She was able to overcome his concerns and make a sale. She has the distinction of being the first woman hired by Stan Melton. Melton was the last of the established real estate companies in Edmonton to end a policy of not hiring women.

Ray Buxton (right) receives a Past President Certificate from President J. G. McAfee, September 1962.
(Edmonton Real Estate Board)

Mabel Gordon, first female director and first female Life Member.
(Edmonton Real Estate Board)

In 1969, Connie Kennedy began her career in real estate. She established the first all-woman company specializing in what was then a new form of residential development: condominiums. Her first project was Hyde Park.

These women were the pioneers who provided the role models for those women who have come into the industry since the 1960s. Women now make up a significant portion of the membership of the Edmonton Real Estate Board. They are active in all phases of the industry from sales persons, to agents, to owners of companies. Their role in the activities of the Board includes membership on the executive, on committees, and in the administration.

National companies

The growth of Edmonton during the golden age also attracted companies from other cities to the Edmonton real estate market. This group included the Vancouver-based firm of Block Brothers and the Toronto-based firm of A. E. LePage. Trust companies also opened real estate divisions. These included Royal Trust, Montreal Trust, Canada Permanent, and National Trust.

These companies sometimes bought existing Edmonton companies and/or recruited Edmontonians to help establish their

operations. Cec Cunningham, an active member of the EREB, was part of this trend. He was born and raised in Saskatchewan. He received his license in 1959 and became involved in property management with his father's firm, Cunningham Agencies. Cec joined Royal Trust's real estate division in 1965. At the time of his sudden death in 1984 he was northern Alberta regional manager and Lendrum branch manager for Royal Trust Corporation in Edmonton. He twice served terms as a director of the EREB and served as president in 1979. He was also a director of AREA and president in 1982. He was awarded a Life Membership by the EREB.

The arrival of Block Brothers was particularly noteworthy. Its aggressive campaign to recruit staff was a new departure for the industry in Edmonton. A. E. LePage established itself in Edmonton by buying the brokerage portion of Melton Real Estate.

The founders of the Edmonton Real Estate Exchange in 1909 created an organization dedicated to the self-regulation of the industry. The collapse of the economy in 1913 made that attempt short-lived. The founders of the 1927 Edmonton Real Estate Association saw the regulation of the industry as a partnership between the industry and government. The passage of the Real Estate Agents' Licensing Act and the ongoing cooperation between the government and the Association made this partnership work.

In 1947 the oil boom gave Edmonton the impetus to grow. The opportunity to build an organization was not missed. Between 1952 and 1981 the Edmonton Real Estate Association was superseded by the Edmonton Real Estate Board and Co-operative Listing Service. The new organization offered a range of services that gave it a great deal more influence within the city and made membership an essential part of being a real estate professional in Edmonton. It was able to establish permanent offices and hire a permanent staff that offered not only a multiple listing service but also educational and social programs.

Edmonton skyline in 1978 had been totally transformed by the postwar boom.
(City of Edmonton Archives, EA-117-149)

CHAPTER SIX

Continuity and Change
1982-1995

Edmonton's longest period of economic growth came to an abrupt end with the 1982 recession. Although the 1982 recession was severe, it is the 1913 recession that remains unchallenged as the real estate industry's greatest crisis in Edmonton's history since the market did not simply decline, it collapsed and remained relatively inactive for years. Northern development projects, such as the construction of a gas pipeline down the MacKenzie Valley from Inuvik to Edmonton, were cancelled.

The 1982 recession caused by the national energy policy was only one of the shocks to the Edmonton economy. The downsizing of all three levels of government has also reduced the number of jobs in the public service sector of the Edmonton economy.

The Edmonton economy has recovered from these events as new projects for northern development are revitalizing its economy. The Board has led the way by adapting to new technologies. It has also played an important role in achieving self-regulation by creating the Real Estate Council of Alberta. The Board has thus retained its commitment to an industry based on integrity while meeting the challenge of change.

Rising expectations

Rising expectations were evident in the Edmonton Regional Planning Commission 1979 Annual Report. It predicted that Edmonton would have a population of a million people by the year 2000. These expectations were based on oil extraction projects planned for Cold Lake and the Fort McMurray area, including the Alsands plant and the MacKenzie Valley pipeline. Construction of the pipeline was estimated to cost $1.5 billion. The ripple effect on the Canadian economy was estimated at $15 billion because of the need for construction materials. It promised to be another Alaska Highway many times over.

The recession of 1982

The recession of 1982 was begun by the national energy policy. It had the effect of directing investment away from the development of Alberta's petroleum resources and towards the frontier regions and Newfoundland. It led to the cancellation of projects designed to develop the oil sands.

Another more long-term factor affecting the Edmonton economy was demographic. The baby boom generation, born between 1946 and 1964, created an unprecedented demand for housing which was not continued into the 1980s and 1990s.

The result of the economic slowdown on the labour force in Edmonton was dramatic. Between 1971 and 1981 employment increased by 165,150 jobs. Between 1981 and 1990 the labour force in the Edmonton metropolitan area increased by only 5,000 jobs. Employment levels in goods-producing industries in 1992 were below their 1981 levels. The largest declines were in construction and manufacturing. Employment growth was concentrated in the service-producing industries.

The impact of the 1982 recession on the Edmonton real estate market was reflected in comments to the press by Art Jones, the then public relations manager for the Edmonton Real Estate Board. In 1983 an article entitled "Grim year for realtors as local ranks dwindle," appeared in the *Edmonton Journal*. While many Canadians were worrying about how wage restraints would affect their lives, the article noted, some Edmontonians were trying to cope with much more stringent constraints. Incomes of the average real estate salesperson dropped by one-third in 1982 because of plummeting sales. In January 1983 Edmonton had 1,820 licensed salespersons, down from 2,388 from a year earlier.

The ranks of the agents were also pared from 353 to 297 because of mergers, closings, and business failures. Low overheads kept small firms in business, while large firms

Canada Place (background) and the Edmonton Convention Centre are two important additions to the east end of Jasper Avenue.
(Edmonton Real Estate Board)

gained strength from economies of scale. Most of the casualties were medium-sized firms. A number of well-established firms went out of business. These included Buxton Real Estate, Weber Brothers, and Graham Real Estate. Two of the exceptions were Spencer Real Estate and Molstad Real Estate.

Despite the situation, Art Jones was still optimistic. In his view, it was a good time to buy a home since interest rates had fallen sharply, there was a good selection of homes on the market, and prices were as good as they were ever going to be. This was especially true of $200,000-plus homes, which had dropped in price by as much as 25 percent.

The negative impact of the recession on the resale housing industry sent the average selling price from $91,405 at the end of 1982 to $74,175 by the end of 1985.

The recession also had a significant impact on land developers. Before the recession, they had amassed large land inventories financed at high rates to avoid a severe shortage of residential lots only a year earlier. Most large developers launched asset reduction programs to dispose of the land and raise cash for other obligations. As in 1913, land purchased on the outskirts of the city was no longer in demand. Murray Fox, vice-president of Carma Ltd., was quoted in the May 5, 1984, *Edmonton Journal* as saying that some of the property: *"looks like it will be farmland for twenty years."* The Nu-West Group Ltd. of Calgary, which sold $330 million in assets, lost $148 million on sales of $683 million in the nine-month period ending September 30, 1982. In the same period in 1981 it earned $12 million on sales of $663 million. Melcor, of Edmonton, also disposed of most of its undeveloped land, and Calgary-based Atco got out of residential construction entirely.

Recovery

But, despite predictions of disaster, the 1980s and 1990s have produced hopeful signs of continued recovery of the Edmonton real estate market from that recession. The average selling price has since reached a high in 1994 of $112,501; but the effects of government downsizing once again pushed prices down in 1995, when the average price was $110,577 at year end. The sales volume also set records early in the 1990s, peaking in 1992 with 12,772 residential sales. Edmonton's population also continued to grow, reaching 626,999 by 1993.

Other signs of recovery are the new projects and upgrades valued at about $3 billion planned for the oil sands industry. As well, the ongoing development of the downtown core indicates economic recovery. New additions include the Eaton's Centre and a convention centre. In September 1991 a new Edmonton Journal Building was opened, replacing an earlier structure built in 1921. In 1993 Alberta College opened Phase One of its new Alberta College campus. This facility has a

250-seat music recital hall, 22 classrooms, and 17 music studios. The college was established in 1903.

The civic centre, begun in the 1950s, was completed in the 1990s with the addition of the Winspear Centre for Music scheduled for opening in 1997. The single most important private donor to the project is Francis Winspear, after whom the building is named. Twelve years of fundraising for its construction and to determine its location were necessary. A new city hall was opened in 1992 to replace the one built in 1956. The new city hall features a plaza that functions as a wading pool in summer and as a skating rink in the winter. Another outstanding feature of the building is a 200-foot (61 metres) $1 million tower with a 40,000 pound (18,160 kilograms), 23 bell carillon that can play up to 99 melodies.

In addition to new buildings, one of Edmonton's landmarks from the pre-World War One boom was restored to its former beauty. The Hotel Macdonald addition, opened in 1953, was demolished, and the original portion completed in 1916 was restored. The restored Hotel Macdonald opened for business in 1991.

The redevelopment of the former site of the Canadian National Railways yards was also undertaken. A new downtown campus for Grant MacEwan Community college was opened on the site in 1993. The new campus provided space for sixty classrooms, twenty-one computer labs, forty instruction labs and other facilities.

Pilot Sound and the Lake District were two new developments during this era. Pilot Sound is a 2,300 acre subdivision in the northeast. Its neighbourhoods are all named after famous aviators. Hollick-Kenyon flew a single-engine plane 2,200 miles across the Antarctic. Matt Berry was one of Edmonton's earlier bush pilots.

The Lake district begun in 1979 continued with the creation of the neighbourhoods of Klarvatten (Swedish for clear water) and Ozerna (Ukrainian for lake area). Water is the theme in this development. Artificial lakes have been created and the neighbourhoods have names associated with water.

A much smaller development is the new district of Dunvegan into which the first residents moved in 1993. It was developed on the former site of the railway yards and depot for the Edmonton Dunvegan & British

Columbia Railway Company. This railway later became the Northern Alberta Railway that was acquired by CN Rail in 1981.

The AgriCom, officially opened in 1984, was one of the new additions to the Exhibition grounds. The first event was a trade show and cultural exhibition held by the People's Republic of China.

Continuity and change in the industry

New suburbs such as Riverbend, established on the eve of the recession of 1982, continued to be developed through the 1980s and 1990s. A town centre was built in Mill Woods and existing malls were expanded and upgraded.

Phases Two and Three were added to West Edmonton Mall. Phase Two, opened in 1983, brought the total number of stores and services to 460. This phase included the world's largest enclosed amusement park and an NHL-sized skating rink. Phase Three, opened in 1985, added a water park. The Hotel was opened in 1986.

The Great West Saddlery Building on 104th Street, built in 1911, is part of the warehouse district that developed south of the Canadian Northern Railway Yards.

(Edmonton Real Estate Board)

West Edmonton Mall offers family attractions such as a waterpark and indoor golfing in addition to a myriad of stores and services.
(West Edmonton Mall Administration)

Many attractions are found at West Edmonton Mall.
(West Edmonton Mall Administration)

Top Left:
This gate on 102nd Ave was constructed in 1987 to commemorate the friendship between Edmonton and its twinned city in China, Harbin.
(Edmonton Real Estate Board)

Top Right:
First Presbyterian Church on 105th Street just south of Jasper Avenue was built in 1911 to serve the needs of a residential population. Today commercial structures and office towers, including the Canadian Utilities Centre (shown to the left of the church), dominate the area.
(Edmonton Real Estate Board)

Bottom Left:
Government House originally served as the residence of the Lieutenant Governor is now used as a government conference centre.
(Edmonton Real Estate Board)

Bottom Right:
The Edmonton Space & Science Centre located in Coronation Park was designed by Douglas Cardinal and opened in 1984. It houses western Canada's first IMAX theatre.
(Edmonton Real Estate Board)

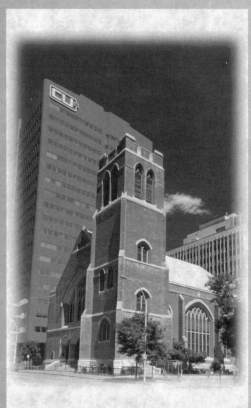

Top: Along with the conversion of land to new uses, buildings in Edmonton during the 1990s were also being converted to serve other functions. The Excelsior Lofts on 104th Street, originally constructed as a warehouse, is now a condominium.

(Edmonton Real Estate Board)

Left and Below: The river valley district of Rossdale is one of Edmonton's older communitites where new construction has been taking place in the 1980s and 1990s. These two developments are located near the James MacDonald Bridge.

(Edmonton Real Estate Board)

Whyte Avenue looking west from the CPR railway tracks in 1996. Unlike Jasper Avenue, the streetscape has remained largely unchanged from its appearance in 1914.
(Edmonton Real Estate Board)

Jasper Avenue looking east from 101st Street in 1995. The Union Bank Building (1910) located on the south side of Jasper Avenue and west of the Telus Tower is the only structure remaining from the pre-World War One boom.
(Edmonton Real Estate Board)

Jasper Avenue looking west from 98 Street as it appeared in 1995. The two oldest buildings in this streetscape are the Union Bank Building (1910) and the Canadian Imperial Bank of Commerce Building (1952). The Union Bank Building located just west of the Telus Tower has been overshadowed by the building activity undertaken since the 1950s.
(Edmonton Real Estate Board)

Another change to the real estate industry, which gathered strength in the 1980s and 1990s, was the appearance of franchises. These national organizations provide opportunities for agents to own their own business. Century 21, which arrived in the 1970s, was followed by RE/MAX in the early 1980s. Realty World, NRS, and HomeLife arrived in the mid-1980s. The Sutton Group was established in October 1989. Realty Executives and Coldwell Banker are from the 1990s. Out of this group, the franchise operation with the greatest impact on the Edmonton real estate market and the Board was RE/MAX.

Bob Cherot and his father owned the western franchise for RE/MAX, a Denver-based organization that began operation in 1973. Cherot opened his first RE/MAX office in Edmonton in 1980. The company challenged the Edmonton real estate community by actively recruiting some of the top producers in the Edmonton market. Many people were attracted to RE/MAX because of its commission concept. Sales people at RE/MAX work on a 100 percent commission basis, paying a monthly management fee and another fee to cover their share of office expenses.

The conventional approach involves splitting the commission between the agent and the sales representative, with the company paying all or most of the office expenses. Block Brothers and Langley Real Estate were two other companies that implemented the 100 percent concept. Other firms studied the approach but some did not make the switch. The 100 percent concept changed the traditional relationship between the agents and the sales representatives.

One impact these national companies and franchised operations have had on the Edmonton Real Estate Board was to change its cohesion, since these organizations held their own training courses and social events. The Board as a social agency was less in demand. A significant reduction in attendance at Board events became evident as the focus turned to stronger corporate allegiances. Doug Balog was president in 1985 and had to deal with these concerns. Given his association with the RE/MAX organization he was caught in the middle of the debate over the value of this trend in the industry.

The inclusion of new homes sales in the MLS® system was another significant development. During the golden age, the home builders had their own sales staff or hired real estate companies to market their houses without taking advantage of the MLS® system. The downturn in the economy was responsible for this change.

Standing committees

Major changes were made to the standing committee system of the Board in 1995 to increase their efficiency.

The Membership Committee continued to recruit new members and evaluate applications for membership. The Arbitration and Professional Standards Committee, which carried forward the Board's traditional interest in maintaining a high ethical standard, had a light work load.

The Education Committee expanded the program of seminars begun in 1970. The current education program ranges from an orientation seminar to many post-licensing courses. The committee also continues to improve the library to ensure that it will complement the education programs.

The Legislative and Public Affairs Committee is increasingly active through direct contact with alderman, MLAs, and MPs in an effort to protect the interests of the public and the industry. Changing the name of the committee to the Government and Political Action Committee in 1991 reflected this new trend. In 1991 the committee initiated a joint meeting between the Board and members of city council as well as meetings with the city administration. The Board appointed a former City of Edmonton Alderman, Olivia Butti, as Advisor of Government Affairs. Her first

The visual identity of the Edmonton Real Estate Board changed over the decades. The first change (second graphic) was a design selected in a Member contest in late 1978. The latest change (bottom) was a professionally designed logo introduced in 1995.

(Edmonton Real Estate Board)

Governmental Affairs Update noted the September 1988 meeting between the directors and the members of the Legislative and Public Affairs Committee with the nine members of council to discuss industry concerns. Topics discussed included acquiring extra computer data and the possibility of involving private industry in the selling and marketing of city property.

The Industrial, Commercial and Investment Committee is also very active. In 1988, the Edmonton Real Estate Board *Daily Bulletin* was changed to give more information on a property. It now provides month-end statistics showing listings and sales of commercial/industrial properties. Sales statistics are compared with sales from the previous year. The *Bulletin* was also reorganized to group properties of a particular type together, such as industrial, commercial, office retail and so on.

New committees included the Managers' Committee and an ad hoc Computer and Technology Committee. The Managers' Committee was established in 1990. It acts as a liaison between the board of directors, managers at large, and salespeople. The second committee managed the implementation of the Stellar II computer system and considers new technology.

Publications

The *Informer* was succeeded in 1986 by a bi-monthly publication, *News and Views.* In 1985 the Board bought the *Real Estate Weekly* from the Bargain Finder Press with the aim of providing members with a low-cost way to advertise. Before 1985 the *Real Estate Weekly* was printed with the agreement of the Edmonton Real Estate Board. The production facilities have been steadily improved to produce a better newspaper at a reduced cost. A desktop publishing system purchased in 1990 was part of this process. This system allows logos and artwork to be scanned into the computer so that full page ads or blocks of smaller ads can be produced inexpensively.

A full-time supervisor was hired and a delivery van was purchased in 1988. The paper is now distributed widely. Press runs by 1995 vary between 27,000 and 30,000. It is distributed north to Athabasca, east to Vegreville, south to Wetaskiwin, and west to Alberta Beach.

The *Real Estate Weekly* provides an affordable means of advertising for the members of the Board. It also informs the public about the industry in general and the Edmonton Real Estate Board in particular, and also promotes the development of Edmonton. It includes information on open houses, city zones, property by type ranging from residential to IC&I, suburban property, and an agency section. In addition to its regular issues, it has also published various specialty issues that are distributed via the *Edmonton Sun.*

Technology

The Edmonton Real Estate Board and its members have always been a leader in Canada in the application of technology. This trend was evident as early as the late 1960s when Buxton Real Estate introduced a two-way radio system.

It permitted the sales representatives to call the office and set up meetings. The use of modern technology has continued with cellular phones, electronic key safes, pagers, computers, facsimile machines, E-mail, special real estate television channels and now the Internet.

The electronic key safe is a timesaver since it is no longer necessary to stop at an office to pick up a key, and it provides increased security for the property owner. The Edmonton Real Estate Board was the first in Canada to use the system, which is made up of three components: entry cards, keyboxes, and a central computer called "LENI," which stands for "Link to Electronic Network of Information." Access to the system can only be obtained by people with the appropriate personal identification numbers. In order to make it more convenient for the seller it can be programmed to restrict access to specific times. It also adds to the security of access by recording the time that an entry is made into

Computer training as illustrated in this October 1992 photograph has been one way in which the Board helped its members keep pace with communications technology.

(Edmonton Real Estate Board)

the building. It has become a standard part of the industry.

Computerization programs initiated in 1978 were continued when the VANDAT system was acquired in 1984. It was originally developed by the Vancouver Real Estate Board and had been made available to other Boards free of charge. In 1987 the system was modified to allow access to tax information by legal description as well as by address. In 1988 City of St. Albert property tax information was available on-line. A new Hewlett Packard main frame computer was installed. The capacity of the VANDAT system to be upgraded to meet the requirements of the Board reached its limit in 1990.

In 1991, during Lorne Clark's presidency, a joint study with the Calgary and Fraser Valley Real Estate Boards was conducted to look at different systems. The joint study meant the boards could share the cost of consultant fees and also increase their buying power. The Computer Committee also visited other centres such as Victoria, Vancouver, and New York to make a better informed decision on this issue. The rapid change in computer technology and the many facets of Board requirements delayed their decision to acquire the Stellar II system until the fall of 1992. The system when acquired was more advanced than any other then in use in North America.

Despite the advantages of the new system and the care with which it was selected, the Stellar introduction early in 1994 was problematic. As Edmonton was chosen for the first installation, members were subjected to the glitches inevitable in a new system. It fell on then-President Stephen Cook to handle the many concerns of irate members. Stephen was able to mediate member concerns while assisting in negotiating beneficial upgrades.

The advantages of the new system included a wider range of information, since new fields were added. The prospect menu, for example, allows the user to locate houses of a particular style and at a particular price in any area of the city within seconds. This program will continue to search incoming listings based on these parameters and will then inform the user. The computer gives the individual real estate salesperson the opportunity to know the market very quickly over a wide area.

The most recent upgrade allows a listing to be entered directly by agents without having to complete a listing input form. This procedure (called "broker load") saves time by reducing the paper work required to make a listing and puts the listing information into the system faster.

Library upgrading

Along with the constant upgrading of the computer system, the library facilities have also been systematically improved and expanded to reflect greater demand for educational materials. New audio/visual equipment was purchased in 1990 so that members could view material on different subjects. The library was also equipped with study desks and a computer terminal, which allows access to the new Stellar II system.

The library resources have been expanded to include videotapes and audio cassettes. These materials include "The Mentor" series by David Knox and "How to be a Winner" by Zig Ziglar. The library also carries copies of legislation relevant to the industry, trade publications, previous copies of the Edmonton Real Estate Board listings and sales catalogues.

Insurance

Bonding had been the traditional way to ensure a person's integrity. Beginning in 1985, bonding was replaced by two mandatory programs that do a better job of protecting the salesperson and the public. The Assurance Fund is administered by the Real Estate Council of Alberta. It protects the buying public from the wilful malpractice of an agent or salesperson. The Errors and Omissions Insurance is operated by the Alberta Real Estate Insurance Exchange, called AREIX. AREIX was introduced in October 1991 to reimburse the public for any agent's errors or negligence. It is a form of liability insurance.

Competition Bureau

The Competition Act is one of the laws passed by the federal government to deal with the maintenance of competition in the market place. The first Combines Investigation Act was passed in 1906. Revisions to that act began to have serious implications for the real estate industry as early as 1975 when infractions under the act were to be dealt with under the criminal code. The Competition Act attempts to police anti-competitive agreements, price fixing, and misleading advertising. The individual boards have voluntarily consented to no fixed fees and commissions, to no restrictions on the services provided by individual members, to not discourage members from offering any type of real estate, and to advertising restrictions and conditions of membership. In their daily business affairs agents and sales personnel must avoid by word or deed even the appearance of collusion. The compliance program is complemented by the well-established efforts of individual boards to develop and enforce codes of ethics to maintain the integrity of the industry. The Edmonton Real Estate Board is a participant in the compliance program and has not been subject to any formal investigations.

Educational requirements

Education continued to be emphasized during the 1980s and 1990s. During this period the primary schools that had been developed by the Board were superseded by Real Estate 1000 and Real Estate 2000 courses. Real Estate 1000 provides sales representatives with an introduction to the industry. Real Estate 2000, introduced in 1984, is the course individuals must take to qualify for the agent's license.

In the 1990s, the educational requirements now include taking post-licensing courses as part of a continuing education program. The Post-Licensing Accreditation Program requires real estate practitioners to take eighteen hours of approved continuing education courses every two years in order to maintain their registration or license. The program began on October 1, 1995, and so eighteen hours of continuing education will be required by September 30, 1997. The Edmonton Real Estate Board offers a full range of courses as part of this program.

The number and range of topics dealt with by the Board's program of seminars has expanded dramatically from the 1970s. The seminar program discusses specialized types of real estate such as condominiums and acreages. Seminars are also being organized that examine various developments in the industry, such as the Prohibition Order and new forms. From time to time the general public is also welcome to register for various seminars. In 1990 the Public Relations Department sponsored the first home buyers' seminar.

Real Estate Council of Alberta

In 1995 the industry became totally self-regulated with the creation of the Real Estate Council of Alberta under the new Real Estate Act. The goal is to promote the integrity of the business and to protect consumers affected by the industry. It also provides services that enhance and improve the industry. It replaces the Superintendent of Real Estate and thus is the administrator of the Real Estate Act.

This act replaced the Real Estate Agents' Licensing Act that had been in place since 1929. The Council is made up of representatives from all of the stakeholders of the industry in Alberta. The Edmonton Real Estate Board is eligible to nominate one representative. Its purpose as defined by the act includes setting and enforcing standards of conduct and examining business practices of industry members.

Ken Shearer played a key role in developing and implementing this new policy. After the Council's creation, he was elected as its first chairman. Ken's contributions to organized real estate have been numerous and significant. Ken joined Melton Real Estate in 1970 and in 1975 became regional manager in British Columbia. In 1982 he became Northern Alberta regional manager after A. E. LePage acquired Melton Real Estate. He was president of the EREB in 1989 and president of AREA in 1994. Ken received a Life Membership from the EREB.

Builders of the Board in the 1980s & 1990s

The strong tradition of leadership brought to the Board was continued into the 1980s and 1990s. The builders of the Board who provided leadership in the 1980s and 1990s include Del Sveinsson, Ron Esch, Harvey Galbraith, Pat Rudiger, and Pat Mooney.

Del has been a REALTOR since 1976. He is a partner and Agent for NRS Haida Realty Ltd. Leduc; actively involved in residential, acreage and commercial sales. Del is a top producer for the industry and a committed volunteer who serves his profession and community. After serving on various committees of the EREB starting in 1980, Del was president in 1983. He has gone on to make contributions to AREA serving as chairman of the Education and Conference Committees and as vice-presient in 1989. From 1990 to 1994 he was chairman of the Alberta Real Estate Insurance Exchange Advisory Board. He has been awarded Life Memberships in the EREB and AREA.

Ron Esch was president of the Board in 1982. In January 1984 he joined the Board as the manager of its Administrative Services Department after having had a very successful career with the firm started by his father. He remained with the Board until 1987 when he became the executive vice-president of the Calgary Real Estate Board.

Harvey Galbraith has played a role in all aspects of the industry. He has been a sales representative, sales and general manager, partner and sole owner, agent and franchise-owner. He is currently president of HomeLife Hargal Realty. His contributions to organized real estate have included serving on various committees and as president of the Board in 1992. During his term he was involved in the research to acquire a new database that would ultimately become the Stellar system. He was also involved in the selection process to replace retiring Executive Vice-President Art Jones. (After an extensive nationwide search, Ron Hutchinson was promoted from the position of Membership Services Manager.) Harvey has also served as a director with AREA. He was REALTOR of the Year in 1994 and received a Life Membership from the EREB in 1995.

In 1979, Pat Rudiger began his real estate career as a licensed salesman for Royal LePage. In 1981 he acquired the RE/MAX franchise in Leduc. In 1986 he was elected vice-president of RE/MAX Edmonton and became Agent/ Manager for Edmonton in 1988. After serving on various committees from 1989 on, Pat became president of the EREB in 1993.

Events during Pat's term included implementing the Plain Language Offer to Purchase Contract for residential properties and the Offer to Purchase and Lease Agreement for the Industrial, Commercial and Investment

Division. (The development of new forms and their revisions has been a major activity of the Board since the formation of the Edmonton Real Estate Association in 1927.)

Another important builder of the Board is Pat Mooney, who began his career with H. R. Kellough Realty Ltd. in 1962. Upon the death of Homer Kellough in 1971, he was part of the group who purchased the company and continued to operate it under the same name. Following the sale of the company to Block Brothers in 1981, he remained with them until 1987. His contributions to organized real estate began in 1982 when he became a director. He was president of the EREB in 1987, a director and president of AREA, and a director of CREA. He was named REALTOR of the Year for 1990, which acknowledges his industry involvement as well as his community activities. He has received Life Memberships from EREB and AREA.

Recent contributors to the operations of the Board include Mary McLean, Sherry Belcourt-Darby, and Heather Gates.

Mary McLean started in the industry in 1974 with the Calgary firm of Toole and Cote. She later worked for H. R. Kellough Realty and Block Brothers. She served as a director for six years and on a number of committees, with Public Relations being the most important to her. During her term this committee organized traditional activities such as the MLS® Golf

Ken Shearer (centre) served as President of the EREB in 1989. He is shown presenting Life Membership to Garf Bennet as Past President Heather Gates looks on.
(Edmonton Real Estate Board)

George Grover, first recipient of REALTOR of the Year Award.
(Edmonton Real Estate Board)

TO

GEORGE W. T. GROVER
F.R.I.

In RECOGNITION of your many SERVICES to your COMMUNITY, your strict ADHERENCE to the REALTORS CODE OF ETHICS and your many CONTRIBUTIONS to your LOCAL REAL ESTATE BOARD

You have been chosen

SALESMAN REALTOR
OF THE YEAR 1960

by the

Edmonton Real Estate Board
Cooperative Listing Bureau Limited

President

Executive Secretary

REALTORS CODE: Do unto others as you would be done by.

Tournament and Family Picnic. A new format for the REALTORS' Ball was also developed. Mary was REALTOR of the Year in 1985 and was made a Life Member of the Edmonton Real Estate Board in 1991.

After leaving her career as a teacher, Sherry Belcourt-Darby started in the industry in 1976. As chairperson of the Education Committee in 1992 she directed the review of the orientation school lecture content, and helped produce an orientation video for new members.

The first woman president of the EREB was Heather Gates. She began her career with A. E. LePage in 1978. Upon becoming a member of the Board, she chaired various committees, including the Sales Representatives Committee, becoming a director in 1985. Heather was given an Honorary Membership in the Edmonton Real Estate Board in 1993 after she moved to Vancouver.

Recognition system

The REALTOR of the Year Award began to be given out regularly in the 1980s. The first recipient of the award in 1960 was George

Grover. George was best known for his efforts to promote education within the industry. The George W. T. Grover Awards of Excellence in Real Estate Studies were established to encourage students to pursue further real estate training at the University of Alberta, Faculty of Extension. In recognition of these contributions he was made a Life Member of the EREB.

Life memberships were awarded to the EREB members judged to have contributed the most to the advancement of organized real estate, who had sustained public confidence in and respect for real estate agents, or who had promoted good relations both within and outside the profession.

George was the first and only recipient of the award until 1981. The Public Affairs Committee suggested re-establishing it. The criteria for achieving the award have remained the same. In addition to those mentioned previously, Brian Macdonald, Taras Chmil, Al Dredge, and Les Philips are other REALTORS whose efforts have earned them this award.

The 1995 REALTOR of the Year recipient was Alec Fedynak. Alec came to Edmonton in 1958 from the Coal Branch area of Alberta. Upon his arrival in Edmonton he obtained a job with Imperial Real Estate. Later he worked for Buxton Real Estate, Weber Brothers, and most recently, A. E. LePage. Between 1975 and 1980 he operated his own company in partnership with Jim Baker.

Alec has been an enthusiastic supporter of the Board. He has served as a director and various committees, the most current being the Political Action Committee. He has served as a governor of the Charitable Foundation and was elected to the office of president in 1995. He received a Life Membership in 1987.

The Board commemorated its own success when it celebrated its sixtieth anniversary in 1987. The celebrations included a banquet and ball, which featured the then-Deputy Prime Minister Don Mazankowski as guest speaker.

Another milestone celebrated by the Board was the burning of the mortgage for the new building. A laser courtesy of the Laser Institute of the University of Alberta was used to burn the mortgage certificate. The ceremony was held on September 11, 1990, in the auditorium as part of an open house that included tours of the building. Bob Buttar was president of the EREB at the time. Bob is following in his father's footsteps, who was president of the

Board in 1962. Bob Buttar joined Haida Realty in 1978 and has remained with them ever since, contributing professional real estate services to the community of Leduc. He has received a Life Membership from the EREB.

The Edmonton Real Estate Board held a high tech mortgage burning ceremony, September 11, 1990. The certificate was ignited by laser.
(Edmonton Real Estate Board)

Social activities

The social life of the Board, while less active than during the golden age, continues to be popular with its members. The current range of social activities includes the REALTORS' Ball, Committee Appreciation Night, Long Term Service Awards Banquet, MLS® Golf Tournament, MLS® Family Picnic, REALTORS Challenge Blood Donor Clinic, and the Annual Christmas Luncheon.

The organization of these events is no longer the responsibility of a standing committee but is coordinated by the Public Relations Department. Of course, individual members continue to play an important role in these events.

The Edmonton Real Estate Board has successfully hosted provincial and national conferences of AREA and CREA. Most recently the EREB hosted the 1995 CREA conference. Its theme was "Focus on the Future." One topic was on the three-month pilot project launched in September where approximately 15,000 properties were listed on the Internet. Through a Home Page established by CREA, Internet users can obtain information, including pictures, from the four participating test sites: Barrie, Calgary, Halifax, and Oakville. The delegates were also informed of the efforts of the Fraser Valley and Vancouver boards to link their MLS® systems.

Staff changes

The most significant change to Board staff was the retirement in 1983 of Norm Winterburn, who had been active in various capacities with the Board since the late 1940s. Art Jones was appointed executive vice-president in his place. Art joined the Edmonton Real Estate Board in 1976 as public relations and education administrator. As executive vice-president, Jones had the challenge of coping with the after-math of the recession of 1982 and the move to the new building.

Art Jones (right) was Executive Vice-President from 1983 to 1993. He is shown here receiving CREA Honorary Membership from CREA President Michael Ziegler in 1992.
(Edmonton Real Estate Board)

He was active in the Executive Officers Council, serving as a member of the Board and as chairman in 1988/89. By virtue of his position with this organization he served on the Board of CREA and was active on many committees with AREA. He has received a Life Membership from the EREB as well as from AREA and CREA.

Art Jones' positive attitude towards the future of real estate in Edmonton and his public relations skills helped the Board make the transition into the post-golden age. His leadership was evident in the ongoing expansions of the computer system.

Ron Hutchinson succeeded Art Jones as execu-tive vice-pres-ident in January 1993,

Ron Hutchinson, Executive Vice-President (right) is shown with 1994 President Stephen Cook acknowledging volunteers at Committee Appreciation Night.
(Edmonton Real Estate Board)

after an intensive nationwide search for someone with both industry and association experience. A native of Assiniboia, Saskatchewan, Ron moved to Edmonton in 1970 after he received a Diploma in Business Administration from the Saskatchewan Technical Institute. He started as a sales representative in 1975 with Weber Brothers Real Estate. He later moved to Canada Trust, where he was a branch manager and training coordinator before starting with the Board in 1986. He was manager of the Education and Membership Department and later manager of membership services.

Restructuring of the Board

In 1995 a report by the Ad Hoc Futures Committee led to the modification of voting rights and the standing committee system during the term of Wayne Moen. The major changes made in the bylaws dealt with voting rights, structure of the board of directors, and the system of standing committees. Under the new bylaws all members after two years of continuous membership will have the right to vote on all matters. The one exception is that sales representative members may only vote for sales representative directors and agents may only vote for agent directors. Agents and agent designates cannot vote for sales representatives. The board of directors is to be made up of four members each from the agents and the sales representatives. These changes reduced the power of the agent members in the organization.

Another revolutionary change was the reduction in the number of standing committees from sixteen to six. The committees that remain are: the Arbitration and Professional Standards; Audit; Government and Political Action; Industrial, Commercial and Investment; Member Services; and Sales Representatives. These committees continue to perform their traditional duties.

Charitable Foundation

The EREB has a long tradition of community service. Before 1987 the Executive Committee had handled requests for donations individually. In 1987, however, the Edmonton Realtors' Charitable Foundation was created.

Now the Charitable Foundation has its own board of governors and committee system to plan specific directions for donations to charities, primarily shelter-related projects.

The Foundation went into operation in 1989 following receipt of its registration number from Revenue Canada. The first chairman was Gary Comrie. Gary began his real estate career in 1967 as a salesman with Canada Permanent Trust Co. For six years he managed its first residential sales office. He then opened an office for Ashford Realty, a division of NuWest Homes. After four years there, he opened his own firm of Comrie-Coughlan Real Estate in 1978. He has served as chairman of the Membership Committee and as a director of the Edmonton Real Estate Board. He was made a Life Member of the Board in 1987.

Interest on Board investments since 1986 was allocated as seed money. The objective was to create a $1 million capital fund. To ensure that such an amount would be accumulated, 75 percent was retained as capital reserves while 25 percent was to be donated. Raising additional funds and accepting donations was expected.

In 1990, a Donor Wall was built to recognize members who have contributed to the Foundation. Engraved brass name plates are used to honour donors who have contributed $100 or more. The Donor Wall also includes donations that have been made in memoriam of others.

The first major fundraiser was a silent auction at the December 13, 1991, Christmas Luncheon. The event was a great success. Over 108 items along with cash donations were received. Net proceeds to the Foundation were $14,147.00, well exceeding the goal of $10,000.

A second fundraiser was a 5-kilometre Classic Run on August 29, 1993. A 3-kilometre Fun Walk, 1/2 kilometre Tots Toddle/Pedal, Mascot Race, and a Corporate Challenge have been added. The events were organized in association with the Running Room. The event was repeated in 1994 and 1995.

The Edmonton Realtors' Charitable Foundation has made donations to the United Way, Catholic Services, Marion Centre, Bissell Centre, and the Edmonton Christmas Bureau. Commitments have also been made to the Youth Emergency Shelter Society and Grant MacEwan College, Senior Studies Institute.

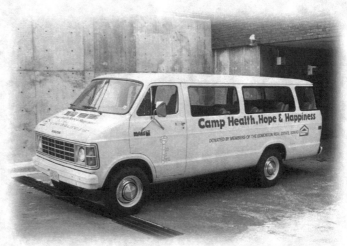

This van was donated by the EREB to Camp Health, Hope and Happiness as part of the activities of the Edmonton Realtors' Charitable Foundation.
(Edmonton Real Estate Board)

Projects in 1992 included a contribution towards the purchase of a lot in the Norwood community to build a home for a needy inner-city family. The official sod-turning for the building of the first Habitat for Humanity home in Edmonton took place on Tuesday, May 26, 1992. In 1993 the Foundation provided funds for the construction of a second home.

At the initiative of the Farms and Acreages Committee, the Edmonton Real Estate Board created a working partnership with the Rural Crime Watch Program. Since sales staff travel widely, they can assist in being the "eyes and ears" of the community and report any suspicious activity to the police.

The Board also sponsored the "Parents against Drug Abuse Program" begun by radio station 1260 and FM 100.3. The "Guide to Fight Substance Abuse" gives valuable information to parents, families, or anyone with a substance abuse problem. The Board distributed 33,000 copies through the *Real Estate Weekly* in March 1992.

The Edmonton Real Estate Board adjusted to the new realities ushered in by the 1982 recession. It is a leader in applying technology to the real estate industry. This is particularly evident in the new computer system. It has also made some fundamental changes to its organization. The Board has reduced the number of standing committees and the two-tier structure of the membership, making agents and sales representatives more equal. The Board has also played a major role in bringing about the self-regulation of the industry through the creation of the Real Estate Council of Alberta. The Board has thus found a new and innovative way of achieving the original goal as stated in 1909 and again in 1927 of maintaining high ethical standards.

Top and Middle Photos:
Enthusiastic runners
and families participate
in The Annual
Edmonton Realtors
Charitable Foundation
(ERCF) Fun Run and
Walk.
(Edmonton Real Estate Board)

Bottom Right Photo:
Graham Downey joins
1994 President Stephen
Cook (right) on behalf
of ERCF in donating a
van to Danielle Larson,
the victim of a violent
crime.
(Edmonton Real Estate Board)

Bottom Left Photo:
Graham Downey
presents a donation to
the Franciscan Sisters
Benevolent Society on
behalf of the ERCF.
(Edmonton Real Estate Board)

Conclusion

The Edmonton Real Estate Exchange of 1909 was the first association of real estate agents and sales personnel in Edmonton that promoted the idea of a code of ethics and a cooperative approach to listings. It was created during an era of excessive land speculation that involved practically the whole community. The real estate industry was inundated during this era by people attracted by the quick profits to be earned.

The creation of the Edmonton Real Estate Association in 1927 was mainly concerned with drafting a code of ethics, which could then be enforced in a formal way through an association working in cooperation with the provincial government. The Edmonton Real Estate Association achieved this objective through legislation that required real estate sales persons to be licensed. The drafting of that legislation and its subsequent enforcement and revision was a cooperative effort between the Association and the provincial government. This was the first step in making the selling of real estate a full-time occupation with professional standards and methods of certification.

Combined with the Association's efforts to establish the real estate industry as a profession were its efforts to protect the role of real estate agents in the community. The need to take action was evident after the First and Second World Wars when the federal government prevented real estate salesmen from earning a commission by selling land to veterans.

During the golden age, progress was made towards self-regulation through a strong Board, the cooperative approach to listings, and the superintendent of the Real Estate Agents' Licensing Act. This objective has been carried forward with the creation of the Real Estate Council of Alberta.

The creation of a co-operative listing service in 1952 was another step made by the industry and the Board. This service gave the Board a central role in marketing property. It provided the information that was essential for success in the industry.

Throughout its history, the Edmonton Real Estate Board has relied on the dedication of its members to staff the many committees that provide direction for its activities. The standing committee system was adopted in 1909. It gave the members control over the organization and was the only approach possible given the economic realities of the Board through to the 1950s. This system has shown its ability to be flexible and get results. The incorporation of new committees such as the Education Committee and the Sales Representatives Committee are evidence of this fact. In 1995 this structure was changed when the committee system was downsized. Changes to voting privileges in 1995 have helped to make agents and sales members equal within the Board.

Since 1909 organized real estate in Edmonton has a number of achievements to its credit. The restructuring of the Edmonton Real Estate Board and the contribution to the creation of the Real Estate Council of Alberta are further accomplishments. Both of these developments reflect new ways to achieve the long-term goal of building an industry with integrity that meets the needs of both the public and members of the industry.

Today, Board members have access to professional development and training specific to the industry. Licensing requirements protect agents and the public alike. A Charitable Foundation, created by the Board, gives thousands of dollars annually to needy local organizations. Social activities are organized to promote friendship and exchange information with other members. A state-of-the-art computer system provides valuable statistics and information to members and the public. Annual awards recognize those outstanding members of the Board who through their dedication and efforts have continued to build on the foundation laid so many years ago.

Alberta is known for its booms and busts, and each cycle has had dramatic effects on the real estate industry. For almost nine decades, however, the Edmonton Real Estate Board, in one form or another, has survived and even prospered. Its ability to change with the times will ensure its continued survival in the future.

Appendices

1927 Edmonton Real Estate Association Code of Ethics

PART I   PROFESSIONAL RELATIONS

Article 1

In the best interest of society, of his associates and of his own business, the Broker should be loyal to the Real Estate Association of his community and active in its work; and he should willingly share with his fellow-members the lessons of his experience.

Article 2

The Broker should so conduct his business as to avoid controversies with his fellow-Brokers; but in the event of controversies between Brokers who are members of the same real estate Association, such controversy should be submitted for arbitration in accordance with the regulations of their Association and not to a suit at law, and the decision in such arbitrations should be accepted as final and binding.

Article 3

When a broker is charged with unethical practice, he should voluntarily place all pertinent facts before the proper tribunal of the real estate Association of which he is a member, for investigation and judgement.

Article 4

A Broker should never publicly criticize a competitor; he should never express an opinion of a competitor's transaction unless requested to do so by one of the principals, and his opinion then should be rendered in accordance with strict professional courtesy and integrity.

Article 5

A Broker should never seek information about a competitor's transaction to use for the purpose of closing the transaction himself or diverting the customer to another property.

Article 6

When a Broker accepts a listing from another Broker, the agency of the broker who offers the listing should be respected until it has expired and the property has come to the attention of the accepting broker from a different source, or until the owner, without solicitation, offers to list with the accepting Broker: furthermore, such a listing should not be passed to a third broker without the consent of the listing broker.

Article 7

Negotiations concerning property which is listed with one broker exclusively should be carried on with the listing broker, not with the owner.

Article 8

The schedule of fees established by the various real estate Associations are believed to represent fair compensation of services rendered in their communities and should be observed by every Broker.

Article 9

A Broker should not solicit the services of any employee in the organization of a fellow-Broker without the knowledge of the employer.

Article 10

No sign should be placed on any property by a Broker without the consent of the owner or his agent.

PART II   RELATIONS TO CLIENTS

Article 11

In justice to those who place their interests in his hands, the Broker should endeavour always to be informed regarding the law, proposed legislation, and other essential facts and public policies which affect these interests.

Article 12

In accepting the agency for property, the Broker pledges himself to be fair to purchaser or tenant, as well as the owner whom he represents and whose interests he should protect and promote as he would his own.

Article 13

A Broker should not buy for himself property listed with him, nor should he acquire any interest therein, without first making his true position clearly known to the listing owner.

Article 14

When asked for an appraisal of real property or an opinion on a real estate problem, the Broker should never give an unconsidered answer; his counsel constitutes a professional service which he should render only after having ascertained and weighted the facts, and for which he should make a fair charge.

Article 15

The Broker should encourage the naming of the actual or an obviously nominal consideration in a Transfer, Agreement for Sale or Assignment.

Article 16

When acting as agent in the management of property, a Broker should not accept any commissions, rebates or profit on expenditures made for the owner without his full knowledge and consent.

Article 17

Before offering a property listed with him by the owner, it is the Broker's duty to advise the owner honestly and intelligently regarding its fair market value.

PART III RELATIONS TO CUSTOMERS AND THE PUBLIC

Article 18

It is the duty of every Broker to protect the public against fraud, misrepresentation, or unethical practices in connection with real estate transactions.

Article 19

Property should be offered by a Broker solely on its merit without exaggeration, concealment, or any form of deception or misleading representation.

Article 20

It is the duty of a Broker to ascertain all pertinent facts whenever possible concerning every property for which he accepts the agency, so that in offering the property he may avoid error, exaggeration and misrepresentation.

Article 21

A broker should never offer a property without the authorization of the owner.

Article 22

The price at which a Broker offers a property should not be higher than that which the owner has openly agreed to take.

Article 23

Before a Broker buys for a client property in the ownership of which the Broker has an interest, he should disclose his interest to all parties to the transaction.

Article 24

Before a Broker sells property in the ownership of which he is interested, he should make it clear to the purchaser that he is acting solely for the owner.

Article 25

A Broker when acting as a Broker should make it clear for which party he is acting, and he should not receive compensation from more than one party except with the full knowledge and consent of all parties to the transaction.

Article 26

Under no circumstances should a Broker permit a property in his charge to be used for illegal or immoral purposes.

Article 27

In closing transactions, the Broker should advise the use of legal counsel when the interest of any party to the transactions appears to require it; and in all cases he should exercise care in the preparation of documents so that they shall embody the exact agreements reached.

Article 28

At the time the agreement is reached as to the terms of a transaction the Broker should fully inform each party regarding commissions and other expenses to which each is respectively liable.

Article 29

Before the closing of a transaction, the Broker should recommend the examination of title and conveyancing papers.

Article 30

All contracts and agreements with which a Broker is a party should be made in writing and should be complete and exact.

Article 31

A Broker should never be instrumental in introducing into a neighbourhood a character of property or occupancy, members of any race or nationality, or any individuals whose presence will clearly be detrimental to property values in that neighbourhood.

Article 32

No instructions nor inducement from any client or customer relieves the Broker from his responsibility strictly to observe this code of Ethics.

502-CA1
Co-operative

No..............................

PROVINCE OF ALBERTA

CANADA

Certificate of Incorporation

I hereby Certify that

...........- EDMONTON REAL ESTATE BOARD CO-OPERATIVE LISTING BUREAU LIMITED -...........

is this day incorporated under "The Co-operative Associations Act, 1946" of the Province of Alberta.

Given under my hand and seal of office at Edmonton this ....- 27th -...........

day of ....- June -........... A.D. 19.52

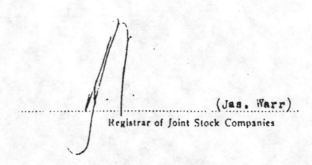

(Jas. Warr)
Registrar of Joint Stock Companies

The Memorandum of Association of the Edmonton Real Estate Board Co-Operative Listing Bureau Limited included ten real estate agents as founding members: M.C. Cummings, J.C. Haliburton, J.N. Winterburn, S.T. Lawrie, J.A. Weber, S.T. Melton, D. Spencer, F. Alloway, W.B. MacGregor, T.C. Visser.

The original document listed the Association's objectives as follows:

To facilitate the marketing of Real Estate by relieving the sellers of the duplication of listing their property with numerous Real Estate Brokers and generally providing a better Real Estate service to the economical benefit of the buyer and the seller.

To promote and foster an educational program for the betterment of the Real Estate profession to the benefit of the buyer and seller of Real Estate

To advance this Co-Operatives movement as a system of business having service as its motive.

Edmonton Real Estate Board Co-operative Listing Bureau

1994 MISSION STATEMENT

An Association of Real Estate professionals dedicated to advancing the quality and scope of service in order to serve the best interests of the profession and the public.

OBJECTIVES

1. To ensure that the Code of Ethics, Standards of Business Practice, Policies, Procedures, Bylaws and Rules and Regulations are in place and adhered to by the members and staff.

2. To continually evaluate member needs, provide effective services and promote their use.

3. To promote the financial viability of the Edmonton Real Estate Board.

4. To ensure the financial viability of the Edmonton Real Estate Board.

5. To continue to raise the standards and improve the levels of education of our members.

6. To continually improve our profile in the community and the public's perception of the Edmonton Real Estate Board and its members.

7. To enhance and promote cooperation and communication among all members and staff.

8. To monitor and influence government activities affecting real estate to ensure that they are in the best interests of our members and the public.

9. To be recognized as the voice of organized real estate in Edmonton and district.

10. To encourage pride in our profession.

11. To promote, encourage, and protect the rights of ownership of real property.

12. To actively participate in the Alberta Real Estate Association and the Canadian Real Estate Association.

1995 CREA Code of Ethics

Under all is the land. Upon its wise utilisation and widely allocated ownership depend the survival and growth of free institutions and of our civilization.

Through the REALTOR, the land resource of the nation reaches its highest use and private land ownership its widest distribution. The REALTOR is instrumental in moulding the form of his or her community and the living and working conditions of its people.

Such functions impose grave social responsibilities which REALTORS can meet only by diligent preparation, and considering it a civic duty to dedicate themselves to the fulfilment of a REALTOR's obligation to society.

The REALTOR therefore must be zealous to maintain, and continually strive to improve, the professional standards of his or her calling:

by keeping informed as to developments and trends in real estate,

by endeavouring to protect the public against fraud, misrepresentation or unethical practice in connection with real estate transactions,

by rendering services and opinions based on the REALTOR's knowledge, training, qualifications and experience in real estate,

by seeking no unfair advantage over, nor injuring directly, the reputation of, nor publicly disparaging the business practice of other REALTORS, and

by being loyal to the REALTOR's Real Estate Board and Provincial/Territorial Association and active in their work.

In the interpretation of his or her obligations, the REALTOR can take no safer guide than that which has been embodied in the Golden Rule — "Do unto others as you would have them do unto you".

No inducement of profit and no instructions from clients or customers can ever justify departure from the ideals of fair dealing and high integrity resulting from adherence to a lofty standard of moral conduct in business relations.

Accepting this standard as his or her own, each REALTOR pledges to observe the spirit of the Code in all dealings and to conduct business in accordance with the standards of Business Practice as adopted by the Canadian Real Estate Association.

Presidents of the Edmonton Real Estate Board

1933-34
N. Roy Weber

1935
Luke Winterburn

1938
Sid Lawrie

1939
Sam Ferris

1940
B. Greene

1941-44
Stuart Darroch

1945
Lou Weber

1947
Mark Cummings

1948
Sid Lawrie

1950
Norm Winterburn, FRI

1951
Don Spencer, FRI

1952
Jack Weber, B.Comm., FRI, SIR

DESIGNATIONS

AACI Accredited Appraiser Canadian Institute	**CCIM** Certified Commercial Investment Membership	**CPM** Certified Property Manager	**CRB** Certified Real Estate Brokerage Manager	**FRI** Fellow of the Real Estate Institute
CAE Certified Association Executive	**CLP** Certified in Land Planning and Development	**CRA** Canadian Residential Appraiser	**CMR** Certified in the Marketing of Real Estate	**SIR** Society of Industrial Realtors

1953
R. W. Grierson, FRI

1954
Stan Melton, FRI

1955
Jack Haliburton

1956
Homer Kellough

1957
Howie Molstad, FRI

1958
Murray Beckhuson

1959-60
Dennis Stewart, FRI

1961
S. G. Scott

1962
Phil Buttar

1963
Ray Buxton

1964
Gordon McAfee, FRI, AACI

1965-66
Ed Shaske, AACI

1967-68
Max Kaplan

1969-70
Mark Dubord

1971
J. R. Sherrin

1972-73
Norm Winterburn, FRI

1974
Trevor Caithness, FRI,
AACI

1975
Harold Dundas, FRI

1976
Norm Murray

1977
Cec Cunningham, FRI

1978
Graham Downey, FRI,
AACI

1979
Jim Baker

1980
Al Scott

1981
Barry Gogal

1982
Ron Esch, FRI

1983
Del Sveinsson

1984
Don Clark, B.Sc., FRI

1985
Doug Balog

1986
Dave Crawford, FRI

1987
Pat Mooney, FRI

1988
Heather Gates

1989
Ken Shearer

1990
Bob Buttar, CRB

1991
Lorne Clark

1992
Harvey Galbraith

1993
Pat Rudger, FRI

1994
Stephen Cook

1995
Wayne Moen

Photos unavailable for the following:

1927-28
Frank Lorimer

1936
John Killen

1929
John Joseph Duggan

1937
Frank Lorimer

1930
H. Milton Martin

1946
J. C. Kenwood

1931
Ralph Blackmer

1949
Carl Orthman

1932
Robert Watson

1949
Tom Magee

Life Members of the Edmonton Real Estate Board

Darrell A. Ball
Murray Beckhuson
Garf Bennett
Bob Buttar, CRB
Raymon Buxton
J. Trevor Caithness, FRI, AACI
Don E. Clark
Gary Comrie, FRI, CMR, CRA
David B. Crawford
Mark Cummings
Cec Cunningham
Graham Downey, FRI, AACI, CMR
Mark Dubord
Harold Dundas, FRI, CMR
James G. Esch, FRI, CMR
Alec Fedynak, FRI, CMR
Harvey Galbraith
Barry Gogal
Mabel Gordon
George Grover, FRI, CPM, CRA
W. Frank Johns, FRI
J. Arthur Jones

Max Kaplan
Homer Kellough
Stan Melton, FRI
Bill MacGregor
Gordon McAfee, FRI, AACI
Ian McKinnon
Mary McLean
Cora Molstad
Howie Molstad, FRI
T. Patrick Mooney, FRI
Norman A. Murray
Earl Pottage, FRI, CMR
Ed Sande, FRI
Edward J. Shaske, AACI
Ken Shearer
J. Sherwin
Don Spencer, FRI
Del Sveinsson, CRB
Jack A. Weber, B. Comm., FRI, SIR
Lou Weber
J. Norm Winterburn, FRI

Presidents of the Edmonton Realtors' Charitable Foundation

Gary V. Comrie, FRI, CMR, CRA	1986-91
Trevor Caithness, FRI, AACI	1991-93
Graham L. Downey, FRI, AACI, CMR	1993-94
Pat Mooney, FRI	1994-95
Alec Fedynak, FRI, CMR	1995-96

REALTOR of the Year

George Grover, CPM, CRA	1960
Brian Macdonald	1981
Dave Crawford	1984
Mary McLean	1985
Barry Gogal	1986
Don Clark	1987
Taras Chmil	1988
Graham Downey, FRI, AACI, CMR	1989
Pat Mooney, FRI	1990
Allan Dredge	1991
Les Phillips	1993
Harvey Galbraith	1994
Alec Fedynak, FRI, CMR	1995

Long-Term Member Recognition

LICENSED AND REGISTERED MEMBERS
OF THE EDMONTON REAL ESTATE BOARD AS OF 1995

25 Years of Service

Brian D. Atkins	Guy C. Hebert	Donald Sabo
Roy B. Avery	Josephine E. Hindle	Emil K. Sabo
Rene H. Blais	Luana M. Houston	Alex A. Semeniuk
Lilli Briske	Marjorie L. King	Ernie Sheyka
Gordon C. Chapman	Hal Kitchen	John J. Sribney
Kevin Coady	Spike M. Kubbernus	Pat E. Stanyer
Gary V. Comrie	Mary Kuchinsky	Benjamin A. Starkman
Orville R. Craft	Neil A. Longson	Nick W. Storoshenko
David B. Crawford	Garnet MacTaggart	Darlene Swelin
Walter Dembicki	Rick H. Molstad	Rein Tammets
James G. Esch	Alex Nashman	Edward B. Towns
Pauline Fletcher	Donald O'Neill	Darryl Trueman
Laureen E. Frey	Melvin N. Pearson	Jerry D. Willes
George P. Frieser	Evan Potter	Janet K. Williams
Harvey Galbraith	Alex Procinsky	Doris H. Woodward
Jerry R. Harlton	Andrew Sabo	

30 Years of Service

Garf Bennett	Calvin J. Krausert
Peter Bohaichuk	Pat T. Mooney, FRI
Stan Chichak	Maurice L. Pellan
Don E. Clark	Earl S. Pottage
Graham L. Downey, FRI, AACI, CMR	Paul Smayda
Fred Flamand	Ruth Thatcher
Grant Hindle	Fiore M. Vecchio
John N. Jimioff	Roland L. Vincent
Ken W. Johnston	Bill Willes
Gerald Koester	

35 Years of Service

Trevor Caithness
Alec Fedynak
Lorne Forsythe
Everett Hagan
Donald R. Penrice
Carlos R. Propp
Ed Sande
Kenneth E. Taylor
John Van Leenen
Roy Warwa

40 Years of Service

Raymond H. Buxton
Grant M. Colquhoun
Roy B. Fletcher
Lucien H. Lorieau
Norman Murray
Henry Perran
Red Rolls
Patrick C. Turner

45 Years of Service

Howard Molstad, FRI

Edmonton Presidents of the Alberta Real Estate Association

1949	Sam Ferris
1951	Mark Cummings
1953	J. A. Weber, B. Comm., FRI, SIR
1955	Stan Melton, FRI
1957	Don Spencer, FRI
1961/62	Gordon McAfee
1964	Dennis Stewart, FRI
1966	Ray Buxton
1969	Phil Buttar
1972	E.B. Graham
1974	Graham Downey FRI, AACI, CMR
1977	Garf Bennett
1979/80	Earl Pottage
1982/83	Cec Cunningham
1983/84	Trevor Caithness
1985/86	Barry Gogal
1986/87	Norm Murray
1990/91	Dave Crawford
1992	Pat Mooney, FRI
1994	Ken Shearer

Edmonton Presidents of the Canadian Real Estate Association

1955	Jack Weber, B. Comm., FRI, SIR
1963	Stan Melton, FRI
1969	Dennis Stewart, FRI
1982	Ray Buxton

Executive Vice-Presidents of the Edmonton Real Estate Board

1959-76	Kelly Haugen
1976-82	Norm Winterburn
1982-93	Art Jones
1993-	Ron Hutchinson

Edmonton Presidents of the Canadian Institute of REALTORS (CIR) Now the Real Estate Institute of Canada

1955	Jack A. Weber, FRI
1968	S.G. McAfee, FRI

Edmonton Chapter Presidents of the Real Estate Institute of Canada

1963, 65-66	E.B. Graham, FRI
1964-65	Jack A. Weber, FRI
1966-67	W.J. Martenson, FRI, AACI
1968-69	Ted Dale, FRI
1969-70	Jim McNaught, FRI, AACI
1970-71	Graham Downey, FRI, AACI
1971-72	Jim Wall, FRI
1972-73	Tom McCaskill, FRI
1973-75	Jack Coughlin, FRI
1974-75	Ernie Drever, FRI
1976-77	Gordon McIndoe, FRI
1978-79	Alec Fedynak, FRI
1979-80	Bob Eilertson, FRI
1980-82	Floyd Farrell, FRI
1982-83	Ian Mellor, FRI
1983-84	Jim Esch, FRI
1985-86	John Mayzel
1986-88	Darcy Frunchak
1988-89	Lillian McLeod, FRI
1989-90	Brian Atkins, FRI, CMR
1990-91	Garry Milne, FRI, CLP
1991-92	Alder Currie, FRI
1992-93	Peter Smith, AACI, FRI
1993-94	Johnson Wong, FRI, AACI
1994-95	Pat Mooney, FRI
1995-96	Pat Rudiger, FRI

Property Profiles

The South West Corner of 101 Street and Jasper Avenue

The legal description of the south west corner of 101 Street and Jasper Avenue is lot 83, Block 1, Plan B. Plan B is one of the oldest subdivisions in Edmonton having been registered with the Government of the North West Territories in July 1882. The plan subdivided all of the land from what is now the north side of Jasper Avenue south to the North Saskatchewan River and from 101 Street to 121 Street. Plan B thus included the area that would become the communities of Oliver and Rossdale.

The plan ignored the geographical realities of Edmonton by creating lots and road allowances which ran down the steep banks of the river valley. The 2,137 lots created by plan B covered only the southern portion of the Hudson's Bay Company Co. Reserve. The creation of such a large number of lots, given Edmonton's small population at this time, was the result of the 1882 land boom described in chapter one.

Owners of lot 83 after the Hudson's Bay Company included Jules Chave and Henri Hetu who were also the owners of the Edmonton Saw Mill Company. In 1895 their interest in this lot along with lot 82 was transferred to George Thomas Bragg for one dollar to cover various incumbrances and liens on the property placed on it by the creditors of the company. The Jacques Cartier Bank, possibly one of these creditors, received title to the land in 1898.

In 1899 the Jacques Cartier Bank sold lots 82 and 83 to the Edmonton businessmen John A. McDougall and Richard Secord for $4,000. In 1902 McDougall and Secord sold these two lots to Leon Bureau, a lawyer from Versailles France, for $10,666.66. Bureau retained ownership until 1905 when he sold them back to McDougall and Secord for $70,000. It was during this period that the Windsor Hotel was constructed at this location.

Between 1902 and 1905 the value of the lots had gone up $59,333.34. This increase reflected the overall growth of Edmonton during the railway boom and the strategic location of this property in the downtown core of the City of Edmonton.

McDougall and Secord retained ownership until June 1913 when the two lots along with other property in downtown Edmonton was sold for $600,000 to Robert McDonald. Given the inclusion of other downtown property in this transaction, it is impossible to determine from the documents available what the cost was of the individual lots. McDonald was the owner of the Yale Hotel at the time of his

purchase of the Windsor. He renamed the Windsor Hotel the Selkirk Hotel in 1914. The Selkirk Hotel operated until 1962. McDonald's purchase of the Hotel coincided with the end of the economic boom. The introduction of prohibition also made the operation of a hotel less profitable. These and other factors prevented McDonald from completing the purchase of the property resulting in its transfer back to McDougall and Secord in 1920.

This is the exterior view of the Selkirk Hotel on the corner of 101 Street and Jasper Avenue.
(Glenbow Archives NC-6-609)

Historical view of the Selkirk Hotel's interior.
(Glenbow Archives NC-6-626)

The two lots were retained by McDougall and Secord until 1950 when they were sold to Mid-Century holdings Ltd. for $440,000.00. The increased value of the land was the result of Edmonton's post-Second World War boom.

On December 16, 1962, the Selkirk Hotel was destroyed by fire. Rather than rebuilding the hotel, the owners sold the land along with lot 81 in 1963 to the Royal Bank for $1,401,000. Subsequent to the purchase, the Royal Bank built an office tower which housed its main branch. The construction of this office tower was part of the post-Second World War rebuilding of downtown Edmonton.

The price of lot 83 thus went up from $2,000 in 1899 to $35,000 in 1905, to $220,000 in 1950 and to $467,000 in 1963.

Current view of the southwest corner of 101 Street and Jasper Avenue.
(Edmonton Real Estate Board)

North West Corner of Whyte Avenue and 103 Street

The property at the north west corner of Whyte Avenue and 103 street is legally described as Lot 1, block 68, Plan I. It is part of River Lot thirteen in the Edmonton Settlement which was originally owned by Thomas Anderson. Anderson was Edmonton's first Dominion land and crown timber agent. He was also the central figure in what became known as "the great land office steal." This incident involved an attempt by Anderson to move the land titles office to the new railway townsite established by the Calgary and Edmonton Railway on the south side in 1891. He was prevented from doing so by the citizens of Edmonton.

Anderson had a personal interest in promoting the new townsite since he had sold river lot thirteen to the Calgary and Edmonton Railway Company. This transaction was negotiated by Augustus Meredith Nanton and John Henry Munson, both of whom were from Winnipeg. The land acquired by the Calgary and Edmonton Railway from Anderson and other owners was subdivided by Plan I. This plan covers all of the land east of 107 Street, west of 97 Street, north of University Avenue and south of Saskatchewan Drive. Unlike plan B, plan I did not subdivide the steep banks of the North Saskatchewan River valley. The plan created 129 blocks of land suitable for further subdivision into lots on land above the valley. Those blocks of land along Whyte Avenue and 104 Street were subdivided into 33 foot lots. The agent for the initial sale of the property in plan I was appropriately named Charles S. Lott.

The land at the corner of Whyte Avenue and 103 Street was the first property developed at the new townsite of South Edmonton (later renamed Strathcona) because it was close to the new Calgary and Edmonton Railway station. A hotel was constructed at this location in the fall of 1891 shortly after the arrival of the railway. Nanton and Munson, on behalf of the Calgary and Edmonton Railway Company, retained ownership until 1904 while leasing the hotel to various individuals. In that year it was sold to Strathcona businessman William H. Sheppard for $5,500.

In 1912 Sheppard sold lots one and two to Joseph Beauchamp and Eliza Chenier for one dollar and other considerations. By 1912 the

The Strathcona Hotel as it appeared shortly after its construction in 1891.
(City of Edmonton Archives EA -157-397)

two lots with improvements were valued at $60,000.

In 1923 the site was purchased by the Presbyterian Church of Canada for use as the Westminster Ladies College. The introduction of prohibition and the postwar depression made hotels a less attractive investment and thus contributed to this temporary change in use. The property was transferred to the United Church of Canada when it was established in 1925.

The building returned to being a hotel in 1928 when it was sold by the United Church to Harrie C.

Pettet for $16,500. Dramatic increases in the value of the property did not take place until after the Second World War. In 1958 Vanguard Holdings purchased the property from the Stampeder Hotel Co. for $190,000 and in 1964 it sold it to the Strathcona Hotel Co. for $275,000.

Exterior view of Strathcona Hotel when it was being used by the Westminster Ladies College. The addition made to the building in 1912 is visible to the north of the building.
(Glenbow Archives NC-6-4651/4652)

The Strathcona Hotel as it appears today. The 1912 addition has been covered with wood siding to make it harmonise with the original 1891 portion.
(Edmonton Real Estate Board)

11220 - 94 Street

The original legal description for the house at 11220 - 94 Street was lot 27, block 28, Plan XLIII. Alexander Rowland and William Humberstone were the original owners of the land in this area. William Humberstone is the best known of the two, since he was associated with the development of the coal mining industry in the Edmonton area.

The land was acquired for the purpose of urban development by John A. McDougall and Richard Secord in 1903. Rowland sold his 132 acres for $16,500 ($125 per acre) and Humberstone sold his 48 acres for $7,000 ($146 per acre). Plan LXIII, registered at the North Alberta Land Titles Office on June 19, 1905, subdivided the land into 1,133 lots, the majority of which were 33 feet in width. The plan included the land north of Rate Creek, east of 101 Street and South of 118 Avenue. In 1906 the Norwood subdivision was extended by the subdivision of additional land to the east. In 1905 when plan LXIII was filed at the Land Titles Office it was outside the existing boundaries of the City of Edmonton.

The Norwood subdivision was put on the market at an opportune time. The Canadian Northern Railway had arrived in that year. The Province of Alberta had also been created and it was expected that Edmonton would become the capital of Alberta. In 1907 McDougall and Secord sold lot 27 to John Billing Radcliffe for $155. Radcliffe was described in the transfer document as a "Gentlemen of the City of Edmonton." He retained ownership of the land without developing it until 1909 when he sold it to Inglis D. Graham, an Edmonton carpenter, for $550. Edmonton contractor Albert Killips purchased the site for one dollar in 1910.

The resale of the property in subsequent years is outlined in the following chart below. The significant trend evident in these statistics is the fact that the value of the property increased by only $14,000 between 1918 and 1972 compared to an increase of $61,500 between 1972 and 1980.

YEAR OF SALE	PRICE PAID
1907	$ 155.00
1909	$ 555.00
1918	$ 2,000.00
1920	$ 3,600.00
1946	$ 4,600.00
1951	$ 7,000.00
1952	$ 9,000.00
1972	$16,000.00
1975	$34,900.00
1978	$56,000.00
1979	$65,900.00
1980	$77,500.00

Current photo of Norwood home.
(Edmonton Real Esate Board)

Current photo of the house at 11028 - 84 Avenue in Garneau.
(Edmonton Real Estate Board)

11028 - 84 Avenue

The house at 11028 - 84 Avenue is part of River Lot Seven of the Edmonton Settlement which was originally owned by Laurent Garneau. He came to Edmonton in 1874 after having participated in the Riel Rebellion as one of Riel's soldiers. In 1901 he moved to St. Paul de Metis where he carried on trading and ranching.

The subdivision of River Lot Seven, which would become the Garneau district, took place between 1899 and 1912. One of the subdivision plans from this period was plan I 23 A. It was registered at the Land Titles Office on June 19, 1905 by Laurent Garneau. It included the land between 83 and 87 Avenues and 110 and 112 Streets. It created four blocks subdivided into 32 lots 50 feet in width and four blocks subdivided into 34 lots of the same width.

Garneau sold blocks 161 and 164 to J. W. Blain, identified on the transfer document as the postmaster of Strathcona, in 1906 for $2,640 or $41.25 per lot. In 1912 Joseph Reid of Kemptville, Ontario sold lots 7 and 8 for

$2,000 to Murray Lister of Edmonton. Lister in turn sold lot 8 to Herbert S. Dean in 1913 for $2,250.00. Dean was responsible for the construction of the house on the lot valued at $3,000. Subsequent sales of the property are noted in the table below.

The trends evident in these statistics are similar to those noted earlier in the profile for the Norwood property. The value rapidly accelerated during the pre-World War One boom. During this period the campus of the University of Alberta was established on the adjacent river lot and the High Level Bridge was completed.

YEAR OF SALE	PRICE PAID
1913	$2,250
1933	$1,800
1957	$10,000
1973	$11,500
1983	$100,000